Praise for Live Unveiled

Cynthia Cavanaugh's amazing Bible study, *Live Unveiled: Freedom to Worship God, Love Others, and Tell Your Story*, draws us deep into who we are, who we are meant to be, and God's desire to bring the two together. We can have more—if we will only seek the truth and believe!

—Anita Agers Brooks, international speaker, inspirational life coach, and award-winning author of *Getting Through What You Can't Get Over*. www.anitabrooks.com

Wondering what's holding you back? Live Unveiled expertly guides you to embrace the life you've been longing for. Through authentic story telling, solid study of the Scripture and practical advice, Cavanaugh invites you on a journey to live fully and with purpose.

—Erica Wiggenhorn, Author of *An Unexplainable Life: Recovering The Wonder and Devotion of the Early Church* and Founder of Every Life Ministries. www.ericawiggenhorn.com

What barriers stop you from living out your very best story? Masks. Lies. I'm not enough? Those words and many more, are veils which taunt us into believing we will never fully achieve the fulfillment and love we are looking for. Cynthia Cavanaugh's 10 week Bible Study LIVE UNVEILED is a gripping and authentic look into finding truth about the woman in the mirror. Cynthia's writing style is engaging and authentic. Each chapter is intertwined with scripture, personal stories and filled with daily challenges for spiritual growth. I absolutely love this Study! It's a masterpiece and should be required reading for every women from age 18-88. Do this Study on your own, or in a group for in-depth discussion. Well done Cynthia.

—Heidi McLaughlin, International speaker and author of 5 books, including *RESTLESS FOR MORE: Fulfillment in Unexpected Places*. www.heartconnection.ca

Embracing who God made us to be—without the shackles of performance—is the epitome of freedom. Author Cynthia Cavanaugh has faced this journey and invites us to retrace her steps as we discover that freedom for ourselves. Every part of this study points the reader back to the foundational truth of God's word. At the same time, Cavanaugh's transparency with the struggles she's faced gives the reader courage to share her own perceived shortcomings and failures and find healing. This is a dynamic, life-changing study and has the ability to rip the veil from our eyes and let us truly see ourselves as God sees us.

—Edie Melson, author of *While My Child is Away* and Director of The Blue Ridge Mountains Christian Writers Conference. www.ediemelson.com

Cynthia Cavanaugh's *Live Unveiled* invites women to study God's word together. The author has tenderly and artfully crafted a delightful Bible study sure to help women grow closer to God through studying His word and guide them through their own difficulties. Offered as an individual or group study, through the author's teaching, women can allow God to peel layers of lies they've believed about themselves. Cavanaugh shares her own struggles with insecurity, unworthiness and shame during her adolescent years when she believed the lie which placed acceptance solely on her appearance. Like so many women, the author made a choice to believe the lie that her appearance tipped the scales toward her acceptance. It took two decades before the author could convince herself that she was valuable and worthy of God's love. Cavanaugh's story is vulnerable, credible and real as it is partnered with the Word of God to show every woman she can trust God with any emotion that may be hindering her from experiencing the abundant life God has planned. Don't live in the shadows anymore! Study the truth of what the God who loves you says and you will be free to *Live Unveiled*.

—Dr. Sheryl D. Giesbrecht
Author of *Experiencing God Through His Names*
Speaker, Radio/TV Personality, Global Influencer
www.FromAshesToBeauty.com

live unveiled

A 10 WEEK BIBLE STUDY

live unveiled
A 10 WEEK BIBLE STUDY

FREEDOM
TO WORSHIP
GOD,
LOVE
OTHERS,
AND TELL
YOUR
STORY

CYNTHIA CAVANAUGH

REDEMPTION
PRESS

Published by Redemption Press, PO Box 427, Enumclaw, WA 98022

Toll Free (844) 2REDEEM (273-3336)

Redemption Press is honored to present this title in partnership with the author. The views expressed or implied in this work are those of the author. Redemption Press provides our imprint seal representing design excellence, creative content, and high quality production.

ISBN 13: 978-1-68314-246-1 (Print)
978-1-68314-247-8 (ePub)
978-1-68314-248-5 (Mobi)

Library of Congress Catalog Card Number: 2017933614

This study is dedicated to my remarkable grandparents, Paul and Melita Ziepke, who are now a part of the "great cloud of witnesses" in Hebrews 12:1. Their journey in life was not easy, but they modeled a passionate love for Jesus. They lived and breathed God's Word every day of their lives, and it is because of their testimony of faith and prayer that I am a follower of Jesus Christ.

CONTENTS

INTRODUCTION

For much of my early adult years, I stuggled with deep insecurities. You would never have known by my smile and vivacious personality. But underneath that smile was a young woman who was lonely, confused, and hurting deeply. At that time, I lived in a beautiful beach community, had great friends, was a new wife, and a mother of a beautiful baby boy. But one day, in all of my confusion, I decided I wasn't good enough to be this boy's mother—and with my hands full of pills and my heart empty, I made a decision that it would just be easier to check out.

What had gone so terribly wrong for me at such a young age? I was ready to call it quits on life, on God, on my husband, Kevin, and my son, Jeremy. My understanding of what it meant to be loved unconditionally was warped by the lie that I had to perform to be accepted and loved, not only by my husband but by God as well.

So what happened, and how did I get to that place? I have a wonderful spiritual heritage, parents and grandparents who passionately lived Christ before me, prayed for me, and loved me to Jesus. I experienced tremendous ministry opportunities throughout my young adult years and served on a short-term mission in Hawaii in which God spoke his calling into my life. Yet even with all of that, I had trouble seeing myself as God saw me, his child, fearfully and wonderfully made, as the psalmist so beautifully describes.

I was constantly evaluating and critiquing myself. I lived and breathed the reality that I couldn't measure up no matter how hard I tried. This came to a climax after I married Kevin and had our first son, Jeremy. The lies escalated to a point where the constant evaluation of myself led to disappointment, despair, and finally, depression.

I ended up by my medicine cabinet, believing the lies that my family would be better off without me. In that moment, as I was standing and holding a handful of pills, Jeremy woke from a nap early—something he rarely did. And as I ran to his room to comfort him, God painted a picture for me. I was like Jeremy standing in my crib, crying miserably, unhappy with life and disillusioned. I wasn't allowing my heavenly Father, my comforter, to reach down, pick me up, and hold me through that confusing time.

Why? Because I believed lies about myself, about God's love for others and for me. It put up barriers so high that I was unable to see clearly my need to unveil myself before God and allow him to enter into the deepest parts of my heart. I was trying too hard to be perfect. It wasn't working.

As I have shared this part of my life's journey with hundreds of women, I have found I am not alone. There is a disturbingly large number of professing Christians who are existing unwittingly in the shadows of Satan's lies, rather than in the freedom that Christ offers in the form of authentic living.

The journey of unmasking has been a difficult one for me, one in which I am still a pilgrim. I share this with you in hopes that you, too, might be free to live an unveiled life—a life full of God's promise and purpose. This study is written out of obedience to what God impressed on me and is born out of my calling and life message.

As you take a few minutes to briefly look through the study, you will find that it is divided into three parts. The first part helps us to identify from Scripture exactly what a veil looks like. It would be hard to unveil if we don't understand what we are looking for.

The second part of the study is where the real digging comes in. It will be tough in some places, and I encourage you to do everything you can to push through all the lessons, and not skip the Scripture. That is where you will find the truth. Take your time. Each week is not a checklist. Each week is designed to help you understand the truth in God's Word for yourself and how applying it can replace the lies you believe. Enlist someone who can pray for you weekly. The best way to experience this study, of course, is in a small group. Processing what you learn with other people makes for a richer and deeper experience.

You might think of the third part of the study as cruising down the other side of the mountain that you have just climbed. Freedom awaits you and me as we embrace truth, learning to walk in freedom and purpose.

I believe in you and more than that, I believe in God, who can help you each step of the way to unveil anything that is holding you back.

It is with great anticipation and encouragement that I invite you to begin a journey of discovery. This is a study that takes great courage, but with the Holy Spirit as your companion, it can transform your heart. That is my prayer.

May our God give you his eyes and his ears to see and hear the truths found in his Word. And may this be the beginning and the affirmation that living an unveiled life is worth the journey.

Because of Jesus I am free,

Cynthia
March 2017

PART I

The Veil

SOUL MIRRORS

DAY ONE

mirror, what do you see? I am not talking about all the things we don't like about ourselves, like the way we wish our noses, eyes, mouths, or shapes of our faces could be different. One of my dearest friends, Cheryl, bemoans the fact that she is 5' 1" and a bit. One day she said to me, "Today I was hoping I wouldn't be short!" I tried not to laugh. I couldn't help but smile at her, affirming the fact I had told her many times before that I thought she was just perfect in every way. Being petite didn't define her as person. Then again, I am nearly six inches taller than she is, so I don't really understand all that she has put up with—short jokes and endless alterations when she buys clothes.

In our extended family, we don't like what we call the "family nose." It's an inside joke, and in a funny way, our trademark. Whether it is our height or a nose, this isn't the reflection I am getting at when I talk about you and me looking in the mirror.

I am speaking about what is deeper, what is underneath—the hidden parts of our soul, our soul mirror, so to speak. Let me ask the same question another way. When you look into the mirror of your soul, what do you see? Or better yet, what do you hope you would see?

To begin our study, we are going to explore what our soul mirrors are, what Scripture defines as the *veils* that can cloud the reflection of Christ in our lives and fog our souls. But before we dig in and get too far, let's look at our key verse within the context of the passage of 2 Corinthians 3.

Therefore, since we have such a hope, we are very bold. We are not like Moses, who would put a veil over his face to keep the Israelites from gazing at it while the radiance was fading away. But their minds were made dull, for to this day the same veil remains when the old covenant is read. It has not been removed, because only in Christ is it taken away. Even to this day when Moses is read, a veil covers their hearts. But whenever anyone turns to the Lord, the veil is taken away. Now the Lord is the Spirit, and where the Spirit of the Lord is, there is freedom. *And we, who with unveiled faces all reflect the Lord's glory, are being transformed into his likeness with ever-increasing glory, which comes from the Lord, who is the Spirit* (2 Corinthians 3:12-18, emphasis added).

1. Take time this first day to read all of 2 Corinthians, chapter 3. Mark in your Bible each time the word *veil* is used.

2. List everything you observe about the word *veil* as it relates to this passage.

DAY TWO

Are you ready? I am amping up with excitement today as we define the word *veil* and look at it from a biblical perspective. Be prepared to find the nuggets that God has revealed in his Word. Take a moment to stop and pray before you begin, asking the Holy Spirit to give you clarity and insight as you study. He so wants to reveal himself to you personally today.

Look up the following Scriptures and note the context in which the word *veil* is used:

Genesis 24:62-65

Genesis 38:13-19

Exodus 34:29-35

Job 22:12-14

Isaiah 47:1-4

From your study of the above Scriptures, create a definition of what you think the word *veil* means:

Now look up *veil* in a dictionary, or other reference, and write the definition below:

How do the two compare or how are they different?

DAY THREE

Years ago we had a little dappled miniature dachsund name Maggie. She was all of about twelve pounds. As I stumbled home weary and exhausted one day, there awaited Maggie. She waited patiently for me to come in the door and set my things down so I could receive the love she wanted to give me. Maggie was full of love and affection. Her big brown eyes would beckon me to relax and remember that life is good and nothing is as wonderful as being loved. Maggie was our faithful companion for almost fourteen years. Her sole purpose in life was to lavish her affection on her family with her ever-playful ways. Maggie couldn't really perform to be loved—she didn't try to cook dinner or wash dishes or clean up after herself—she was an expert at just "being." And that is why we loved her so.

Sometimes, I wish I could be more like Maggie—carefree in my giving and receiving of love to others. It has taken me most of my life to understand some basic truths about receiving love, especially the love of our heavenly Father. Somehow in the midst of my childhood, I acquired the notion that in order for me to be totally loved and accepted, I needed to perform, to earn, and to achieve.

The harsh reality of this lie was thrust on me one day as I was coming home on the bus from school. I was in seventh grade and was by no means a beauty. I was in that awkward in-between stage of a child becoming a young adult woman. I had resigned myself to being ordinary, with ordinary looks and personality for a fourteen-year-old. As we approached the bus stop closest to my house, a fifteen-year-old boy who was known to be a troublemaker, stood up before the whole bus and pointed directly at me. He proceeded to declare in a voice that I felt sure the whole world could hear, "You are so ugly!" The bus erupted in laughter and I couldn't get off that bus fast enough.

The final two minutes of that bus ride seemed like hours. I wished I could have disappeared as the comments and laughter flooded through my head. I ran off the bus to an empty house, threw myself on my bed, and cried the rest of the afternoon like a teenage girl does with out-of-control hormones running wild. I remember thinking,

Of all the girls in the world, why did I have to be ugly? Something changed in my heart that day because I believed that silly boy.

I believed the lie that placed acceptance squarely on my appearance. Satan won that day in my mind as I made a choice to believe the lie that my appearance tipped the scales away from my acceptance. This ugly lie crippled me well into my adult years. The more I nurtured it, the more it took root. I didn't have anyone to talk to about what happened that day. I was alone and I felt embarrassed and ashamed to even tell anyone what happened for a long time. So I kept it to myself, and the lie grew.

Much of my behavior and what I believed in the following years was done so I could convince myself that I was valuable and worthy of God's love. When I failed others or myself, depression crept in. The shame of that day haunted me. The sting of rejection beat out the truth.

It took a few decades for me to recognize just how I had allowed that moment in time to determine my destiny. I am almost ashamed to admit it because I know that many women face more difficult issues in their childhoods, such as the horror of sexual abuse. I allowed a phrase of words on that bus to move me to a place of deep insecurity, which put me smack into a stronghold of false beliefs. It became a comfortable veil until Jesus met me and helped me to remove both it and the lies that had been embedded for too long.

In the course of my healing journey of overcoming the lies and the depression that accompanied it, Psalm 139 became a treasure to me. By taking the time to unpack this psalm in its entirety, we become totally in awe of God our Creator. He is an intentional Designer. You and I are marvelously created human beings; we have worth and value because we have been made in the image of God.

Read Psalm 139. As you read, make a list of what God says about you.

Now personalize these verses by inserting your name in the blanks, and then read them aloud to yourself:

For you created _____'s inmost being.

You knit _____together in her mother's womb.

Verse 14 - _____praises you because she is fearfully and wonderfully made; your works are wonderful; _____knows that full well.

Verse 15 - _____'s frame was not hidden from you when _____was made in the secret place.

When_____was woven together in the depths of the earth,

Verse 16 - Your eyes saw _____'s unformed body.

All the days ordained for _____ were written in your book before one of them came to be.

My prayer for you today is that after reading this psalm and personalizing it, you can praise God because you are fearfully and wonderfully made! Choose to believe what God says about you no matter what has been spoken over your life. As you close today's study, take a moment and do exactly what this psalmist declares. Write a prayer of thanksgiving for who he made you to be! Don't skip this part today. Ask God to help you find the same things that he so loves about you and write them out.

DAY FOUR

Yesterday we looked into our soul mirror and saw that God has created us fearfully and wonderfully. Understanding our worth and value before God is critical to living an unveiled life. It's part of being on the receiving end of God's unconditional love toward you and me.

Today we are going to take this concept a step further as we compare what God's Word says against what our culture dictates to us about our value before God.

Read the following verses and note what God says about you:

Ephesians 2:9-10

Jeremiah 31:3

Galatians 3:29

Think about what you hear or see on television, read in a magazine, or observe when you are out in your community. What are some of the messages that we receive from our culture about our value? List at least five.

1.

2.

3.

4.

5.

Now go back over this list and circle the ones that you have believed either recently or in the past. What is one thing you can do this week to tackle the most difficult lie you are believing about your own value?

When was the last time you purchased or did something based on the message of an advertisement? What did you buy? Why did you buy it?

Now list what you know to be true from God's Word. Use the concordance from your Bible or an exhaustive concordance, like Strong's, to find verses that support your findings. Here are a few internet resources you can use to dig a little deeper: www.biblegateway.com or www.blueletterbible.org.

As we close our study today, spend some time talking to God about those cultural lies. Ask him to help you identify which of them has been keeping you from believing God and all that he has for you and your future.

DAY FIVE

There are hundreds of verses in the Bible that affirm our worth to God. If we are to be all that God intends us to be, we must acknowledge and claim the promises we find in the Bible. Sounds simple enough, doesn't it? It's the only thing that really works! His Word is powerful and alive in our lives when we claim it.

As we finish up this week and begin to look into our soul mirrors, I encourage you to choose two or three promises that we've studied this week and/or promises you discover and write them out and put them in a place where you can be reminded daily of God's great love for you.

To refute the lies, we have to replace them with God's truth, and wallpapering your mind with God's Word is the only way to overcome the lies that we believe about our own value. Trust me, it works. The more we apply truth, the further and further the lies drift and we begin to believe the truth. Remember, "You shall know the truth and the truth will set you free" (John 8:32).

I am believing with you as we embark on this journey together and am praying for God to reveal himself to you personally as you seek his Word in prayer and study!

Reflection

For you created my inmost being; you knit me together in my mother's womb.
I praise you because I am fearfully and wonderfully made; your works
are wonderful, I know that full well. My frame was not hidden from you
when I was made in the secret place. When I was woven together in the
depths of the earth, your eyes saw my unformed body. All the days ordained
for me were written in your book before one of them came to be (Psalm 139:13-16).

Week Two

CELEBRATING
THE DESIGN

DAY ONE

Last week we explored what a veil was by looking through Scripture. We also started the process of understanding the importance of seeing our value and worth before God as we peer into our soul mirror.

This week I would like to take us a step deeper as we focus on *celebrating the design*. One of the reasons I think we have a hard time celebrating our design is a lack of understanding of how God made us—the remarkable truth of each person's life.

Since the beginning of history, our culture has robbed you and me of the truth of understanding who and what God is all about and the incredible faithfulness of his unconditional love towards us. As a potter creates a beautiful pot, God has molded each one of us in a distinct way that is consistent with who he is. And each of us has a purpose for our lifetime and the impact we potentially will make on human history. Do you believe that? Or do you believe that your life is merely a fleeting moment in time, of limited impact or value?

I would like to suggest to you that God uses the three components below in molding us for his purpose. We are going to look at the first two in our study this week and leave the third one, which is giftedness, for later. Once we understand how God shapes us, we are able to explore the gifts he has given us. That's another topic of discussion and there is enough material available about it to write another study. I've included some resources at the end of the study if you want to explore this further, but for now let's tackle the first two.

Our relationship to Christ
Our life experiences
Our giftedness

Look up the verses below and note the aspects of our relationship to God. What are the necessary components of our relationship with him?

Psalm 13:5

Psalm 91:16

Psalm 116:13

Psalm 118:21

Psalm 119:166-167

Titus 2:11-14

Philippians 2:12

Ephesians 1:3

John 1:10-13

God's original plan was and still is to have a relationship with us. Apart from him, we mirror nothing but ourselves—no power, no effectiveness for eternity. That relationship with him is vital! Our ability to have a relationship with him is part of the design that we can celebrate.

Look up Philippians 1:3-6 and complete the sentence:

I thank my God every time I remember you. In all my prayers for all of you, I always pray with joy because of your partnership in the gospel from the first day until now, being confident of this, that he who _____ a _____ work in _____ will carry it on to _____ until the day of Christ Jesus.

Sometimes our relationship feels like it is faltering and this verse is a good reminder that our relationship with God is a process. This is why our salvation is so important. Because of the sacrifice of God's Son Jesus Christ, we are able to enter into a relationship with him, sinful as we are. He paid the price for us to have the benefits of a meaningful relationship with him.

Maybe you are in this study and haven't yet figured out what it means to have a true relationship with Jesus Christ. Maybe you have unanswered questions. I would encourage you at this point to seek out someone you can talk to and get some answers from. Focus on the Family has a great resource on its website to help you start your journey. Here is the link: http://www.focusonthefamily.com/faith/becoming-a-christian.

The New Testament book of John is a great place to start reading to answer your questions about what it means to follow Christ.

As we close today's lesson, evaluate where your relationship with Jesus is right now. Talk to him about it and take steps to get back on the right track if you are struggling. Admit your need for him and ask his forgiveness if you have been staying away from the relationship. It doesn't change his love for you. He is waiting for you right now and welcomes you lovingly.

DAY TWO

The second component God uses in molding us is our *life experiences*. While we can share similar experiences, like snowflakes, there are no two people exactly alike. Our distinct characteristics are molded by God—the joys, triumphs, and tragedies. The valley and mountaintop experiences distinguish us from one another and allow us to be effective in specific ways with the people God brings through our sphere of influence.

For the next two days of our study, I am inviting you to participate in an exercise that I believe can help you see the big picture. Our life experiences can radically affect our world around us as they are viewed through our relationship with Jesus Christ.

For today, on a separate sheet of paper, list a sequence of people and significant events that chronologically depict your life. You can either begin in the present day and work back or from the time you were a child looking forward, whichever works for you. Don't worry too much if they are out of order. Just write down what comes to mind for you. For example:

> Born_____ in California
> Moved to _____at age three
> Aunt _____ spent summers with me
> And the list goes on …

There may be some events in your life that you haven't thought of or referred to in years because of the pain associated with them. I'd encourage you to include them in the list anyway, because undoubtedly God's plan for that pain is relevant for the direction in which he is leading you. And no pain is ever wasted—I really have witnessed this in my own life and the lives of others.

If you have very painful memories related to abuse of some kind that you have not sought help with, maybe now is the time for you to share your story with a godly counselor and begin the journey of healing from those memories.

DAY THREE

Now that you have chronologically listed the people and events in your life, put these events into a story. As you write, many details and events will come rushing back, including people and incidents you have not thought about for years. Here are some helps in determining what should be included in your story:

As you write, include:

The *events* of your life that have had an impact on who you are today.

The *people* who have influenced and shaped your life.

The *significant* circumstances that affected your life direction, including any incidents or statements made about you before your birth.

Your story should represent the highlights of your development as a person. Include those things that you think are significant and help give an overall picture of your life. Do not pressure yourself. This is for you to see and use. Challenge yourself to be open and honest.

Examples:

> People – parents, friends, teachers, etc.
> Events – graduation, marriage, birth of child, new job
> Circumstances – conflict with parents, place of growing up

My story …

DAY FOUR

Take your written story and transfer the people, events, and circumstances you wrote about and make a timeline on the following blank page. There is a sample at the end of the book of my own timeline and I chose to put it into a chart to make it easier to view. You will notice that I took it a step further by using a table to indicate chapters and then identifying the different seasons and giving them a name with a lesson learned. You can make it as simple or elaborate as you wish, using a chart or a line from your creavity; however, the goal is to finish it!

Start by listing chronologically the people, events, and circumstances in your life and then transfer them to your timeline or chart.

Life experiences

⟵———————————————————————————⟶

People

parents, friends,
teachers, leaders,
contacts

Events

marriage, loss,
achievements,
births, crises

Circumstances

seasons of life,
storms, assignments

My timeline:

DAY FIVE

I hope you were able to see a little bit of the big picture God sees when he looks at your life. This exercise was life changing and affirming for me as I have sought to understand God's purpose and will for my life. Our understanding is so limited but we can trust our heavenly Father who is our guide on this journey we call life.

To close this week, I have listed some questions to help you scrutinize your timeline, questions that may stir some of you deep within. I encourage you to take heart and lean into reflecting during this time. I will be praying for you as you explore these questions for your own life.

Discovering the future

People who know me well believe I am most used by God when I am involved in _____ Why?

When I think about doing something for God in the future, I would love to focus on_____ Why?

The character qualities that I most admire and desire for God to mold into my life are _____ Why?

The person in my life who I believe is having or has had the greatest impact would be _____ Why?

If there is one thing my timeline reveals, it shows that I am often called upon by God to _____ Why?

When people talk about their passion, I often begin to think about giving my life to accomplishing _____ Why?

(This exercise has been adapted and taken from training/teaching learned from CRM/Walling2000.)

Reflection

For it is by grace you have been saved, through faith—and this not from yourselves, it is the gift of God—not by works, so that no one can boast. For we are God's workmanship, created in Christ Jesus to do good works, which God prepared in advance for us to do (Ephesians 2:9-10).

PART II

Identifying the Veils

Week Three

PERFORMANCE OR PURPOSE

DAY ONE

This week we are going to roll up our sleeves and begin the real work of looking into our soul mirror for the veils that may have crept into our lives. Let's start with an illustration to which I think most of us can relate.

I consider myself a fairly good housekeeper, but I have a few hidden closets and drawers that never seem to get organized. There are days when I know I should tackle them, but when I get near a particular closet or shelf, I want to shut it quickly and run away! I'd sooner run to find something more creative or interesting to do like cooking up a batch of my favorite chocolate chip cookies!

I often feel the same way in moments when God asks me to look into my soul because there is something that seems to be clouding up his reflection in my life. At times I just want to scream and ignore the Lord's prompting and instead do something more comfortable spiritually—like read a devotional or start a new ministry. But the Lord gently calls me back and invites me to be obedient.

I can remember one New Year's Eve when I was journaling. I asked the Lord to reveal to me the hidden parts of my character that needed some work and to do whatever it took to clean it up.

My advice to you is this: *Never* pray such a prayer unless you are ready and willing to accept the mission. The Lord definitely answered my prayer and that year was challenging as I leaned into his work in my heart and life.

Recently, at the start of this new year, he has shown me clearly that there is a part of my character that isn't very disciplined. I can show incredible stamina in some areas, but in others, such as exercise or going to bed on time and not staying up so late, I tend to give in to how "I feel" at the moment.

Needless to say, I am asking God to bring this to the front of the line when it comes to practicing greater discipline. I am working on not listening to my feelings so much in that area and toughening up to discipline myself. That's what working on our character looks like, being intentional and allowing the Holy Spirit to help us become self-aware in an area that needs cleaning up.

For the next three weeks of our study, we will do just that—ask God to help us remove those veils that are keeping us from reflecting his glory and the things that nag away at our character. Hang on tight and know that as God leads, he will be faithful to complete the process. I am right here with you.

In Part I of our study, we explored what a veil is and what it looks like. For review, write your own definition of the word *veil* and what you learned about it from your study:

Read Exodus 34:27-35. Why did Moses put the veil back over his face?

Read again 2 Corinthians 3:12-18. Now read this same passage below in a different translation:

With that kind of hope to excite us, nothing holds us back. Unlike Moses, we have nothing to hide. Everything is out in the open with us. He wore a veil so the children of Israel wouldn't notice that the glory was fading away—and they didn't notice. They didn't notice it then and they don't notice it now, don't notice that there's nothing left behind that veil. Even today when the proclamations of that old, bankrupt government are read out, they can't see through it. Only Christ can get rid of the veil so they can see for themselves that there's nothing there.

Whenever, though, they turn to face God as Moses did, God removes the veil and there they are—face to face! They suddenly recognize that God is a living, personal presence, not a piece of chiseled stone. And when God is personally present, a living Spirit, that old, constricting legislation is recognized as obsolete. We're free of it! All of us! Nothing between us and God, our faces shining with the brightness of his face. And so we are transfigured much like the Messiah, our lives gradually becoming brighter and more beautiful as God enters our lives and we become like him (msg).

What do you observe about Moses from this passage from THE MESSAGE Bible?

What promise is given regarding the old covenant?

We have the privilege of living under the new covenant. And because of the work that Jesus Christ did on the cross, we also have access to the Holy Spirit's work in our hearts. We have the liberty in Christ to be free from our sinful patterns and desires that keep us from living out our full potential for the Lord.

Since we have come to understand that a veil conceals and disguises, our desire then is to have nothing that would keep us from that freedom in Christ as this passage suggests.

Let's look at three possible veils (there are many more!) that can keep us from experiencing the freedom that is ours in Christ Jesus. This week we are going to look at the Veil of Performance v. Purpose.

As we close today, spend a few minutes reflecting and ask the Lord to open your heart to what he would desire to have you learn these next weeks. Ask him to give you a willing mind, heart, and spirit to confront those areas in your life that need confronting.

Write it out in a prayer below.

DAY TWO

As I have confessed to you already, most of my life I have struggled to see myself as God sees me and understand that he has truly and distinctly molded me for his purposes. I know I am not alone and that many women struggle with these same issues. And we compensate for these feelings by "doing." We "do" as a means to gain the love and acceptance that is so desperately missing from our lives. We do "over and above" for our families, our jobs, our churches, and our friends, thinking if we perform harder and longer we will earn God's affection. Wearing the veil of performance means being driven to be accepted by others, being people pleasers and doing anything and everything for approval.

Performance has been a significant stronghold in my life and it crippled me in areas I didn't even recognize until God freed me from it. It wasn't until I really focused on the truth of God's Word that I was able to confront the battle with the enemy, Satan. He has been whispering lies to me for years and I wasn't even aware of how deep those lies had lodged in my soul.

Read once again 2 Corinthians 3:16 and fill in the blanks.

But whenever _____ turns to the Lord, the _____ is _____ _____.

Now the Lord is the Spirit, and where the _____ ____ _____ _____ is, there is

_____.

What a profound passage of Scripture! As we turn to the Lord, the veil is taken away! Turning to the Lord so the veil can be taken away means we need to identify our performance issues and meet them head on. Performance issues begin with the lies we believe about ourselves. Take a few minutes to identify your own lies through this questionnaire:

What are my lies? questionnaire

Read each statement and indicate your agreement/disagreement by using the following scale:

1	2	3	4	5	6	7
Strongly			Neutral			Strongly
disagree						agree

Do not spend too much time on any one statement, but give the answer that best describes how you really feel. Try to avoid using the neutral (4) response.

____1. I must be perfect.

____2. I must have everyone's approval.

____3. It is easier to avoid problems than to face them.

____4. Things have to go my way for me to be happy.

____5. My unhappiness is externally caused.

____6. I can have it all.

____7. I am only as good as what I do.

____8. Life should be easy.

____9. Life should be fair.

____10. I shouldn't have to wait for what I want.

____11. People are basically good.

____12. My marriage problems are my spouse's fault.

____13. If my marriage takes hard work, my spouse and I must not be right for each other.

___14. My spouse should meet all my needs.

___15. My spouse owes me for what I have done for him/her.

___16. I shouldn't have to change who I am in order to make my marriage better.

___17. My spouse should be like me.

___18. I often make mountains out of molehills.

___19. I often take things personally.

___20. Things are black and white to me.

___21. I often miss the forest for the trees.

___22. The past predicts the future.

___23. I often reason things out with my feelings rather than the facts.

___24. God's love can be earned.

___25. God hates the sin and the sinner.

___26. Because I'm a Christian, God will protect me from pain and suffering.

___27. All of my problems are caused by my sins.

___28. It is my Christian duty to meet all the needs of others.

___29. Painful emotions such as anger, depression, and anxiety are signs that my faith in God is weak.

___30. God can't use me unless I am spiritually strong.

Each of the statements in this list is a lie or a way that we lie to ourselves. Thus, the more you agreed with each statement, the more you are agreeing with a lie. Go back through your responses and put a check mark by any statement that you marked with a 5, 6, or 7. These are the lies that you tend to believe the most and the ones to which you need to pay the most attention. To defeat a lie, you need to pray and bind Satan with the truth of Scripture.

(From *The Lies We Believe* by Dr. Chris Thurman, Thomas Nelson Publishers, 2003.)

Write down the three most prominent lies that showed up or any others the Lord has revealed to you as you've gone through this exercise. Spend some time talking to God about it and ask him to replace those lies with promises from his Word. If what you've discovered in this exercise concerns you, I'd recommend that you spend more time researching and/or getting godly counsel on these issues.

DAY THREE

The opposite of living a life veiled by performance and being driven is to live a life of purpose. What do the following passages say about our primary purpose?

Matthew 28:18-20

Mark 12:30-31

Jesus clearly understood his purpose. He wasn't tossed around by what the culture dictated to him. He had a clear vision and mission for his time here on earth.

Read John 17 and note what he says his purpose was when he was here on earth.

What does Jesus say about his heavenly Father?

List the things Jesus wanted to pass on to the disciples before he left.

Jesus clearly knew what he was to do. Verses 1-5 explain his mission. Our purpose, as we have discovered in our theme verse in 2 Corinthians, is to brightly reflect the glory of God. But if we are driven to please others instead of God, running around in a half-crazed mode at times, the performance veil is shrouding the glory of the Lord.

Think back over the last week. How much of what you did was driven by the veil to please others instead of God? Be specific and name those actions.

As we close today's study, bring your veil of performance to the Lord and ask him to help you overcome it the next time. Write a prayer expressing your heart to him. If you need some help with such a prayer, I've given you a sample:

Lord Jesus, I have discovered that my life has been shrouded by the veil of performance. I have believed that what I accomplish is more important and more valuable than who I am. I understand now that this is a lie. I repent of this sin and ask that you break any strongholds this lie has created in me. Father, I ask you to show me clearly when I am operating in this mode. My desire is to be authentic, both before you and before those around me, so Holy Spirit, I am asking you to do a work of forgiveness and healing in my heart. In Jesus' name, amen.

DAY FOUR

One of the clearest ways to understand our purpose for each day—loving God and others—is to practice the disciplines of slowing down, being quiet and still, and reflecting. Jesus understood this clearly. Read the following passages and make notes on what Jesus did before and after he spent time in solitude.

Matthew 14:13-23

Mark 1:32-37

Luke 5:12-16

These passages refer to Jesus retreating to a solitary place to pray and be quiet. Sometimes our problem is that we think we can do it better than Jesus can, we think we are the fourth member of the Trinity, as I heard one of my favorite Bible teachers Howard Hendricks say once at a leadership conference.

How ludicrously blind it would be to conclude that our ministries can be purposeful and effective if there is never a scheduled time to refuel or recharge emotionally, physically, and spiritually. Overall wholeness of a person is critical for effective living, so to fall into the performance trap is hazardous to our lives.

Read Psalm 46:10 and write out what you think it means to "be still and know."

As we close today, let me share a quote with you from Mother Teresa:

"We need to find God, and he cannot be found in noise and restlessness. God is the friend of silence. See how nature, trees, flowers, grass—grows in silence, see the stars, the moon and the sun, how they move in silence … we need silence to be able to touch souls."

DAY FIVE

As someone who has struggled greatly with performance issues, I understand that being still and quiet will be a difficult discipline to learn. It seems much more natural and productive to "do" rather than "be." Learning to be obedient in this area has brought much reward and, believe it or not, the ability to look forward to those times of being still before God. I would be dishonest if I told you I have mastered this area of my life. I know I will always be challenged with the choice of "to do" or "to be." But the reward and joy of being obedient far outweigh the consequences of constant hurry and being task driven.

The Bible is very serious when it speaks about "rest." Look up the following passages and make note of what God says about *rest*.

Exodus 35:2

Isaiah 57:20

Hebrews 4:1-11

Psalm 62:1

Psalm 91:1

Proverbs 6:10

Jeremiah 6:16

Matthew 11:28

Removing the veil of performance is difficult work; it means trading in your "to do" badge for your "to be" badge. An incredible revelation came to me when I was working through this process: I didn't have "to do" it on my own. As I confessed my need and my struggle before the Lord, he was faithful to help me overcome it. I am confident that he can do that for you too as you lean in and surrender!

In the time you have remaining today, find a quiet place and rest in his presence. Listen to some worship music, read and journal a passage of Scripture back to the Lord as a prayer, and then just sit and be quiet before him and *listen* in the quietness. What is he saying to you? Enjoy your relationship with your friend and Savior; bask in his everlasting love. I pray you will find peace and rest in your spirit.

When you are finished, write down your impressions of your time with God.

Reflection

My soul finds rest in God alone; my salvation comes from him (Psalm 62:1).

SECRECY OR TRANSPARENCY

DAY ONE

Remember the game we used to play as kids, hide and seek? Someone would be sent out of the group to count behind a tree while the rest would hide, and then the counter would try to find those hiding. Unfortunately, adults still play this game, only it's a little more complicated.

Some are hiding behind walls or bushes or trees, not coming out in the open and letting others see them for who they are—not letting others love them entirely because the walls of secrecy are up. Do you know people like this?

The walls of secrecy go up for many reasons. Sometimes it is because we have been wounded by others and vowed never to open up again and be intimately known. It is not without validity that woundedness creates walls. It is a great risk to be transparent. Misunderstanding and hurt are nearly inevitable. Every one of us has a desire to be loved, known, and understood. This is one of the great mysteries of the human race—the desire within us to know and be known conflicting with the unwillingness to be authentic. This is the next veil we are going to look at, the veil of secrecy.

The dictionary defines the word *secrecy* as the condition of being hidden or concealed; the habit or practice of keeping secrets or maintaining privacy or concealment. It also gives the meaning of being clandestine or even suppression. Let's see what the Bible has to say on the subject of secrecy. Look up the following verses and note your observations.

Psalm 90:8

Jeremiah 23:24

John 18:20

Ephesians 5:12

After reading and making notes on the verses about secrecy, what is your impression? Write out a definition from what you have gathered so far.

DAY TWO

I love the classic story of *The Velveteen Rabbit*. It is a story about some nursery toys and a little boy. When the little boy is fast asleep, the toys come to life and two in particular carry on a conversation. The little velveteen rabbit is new to the nursery and there is a wise toy, the Skin Horse, who has been there for a long time. The Skin Horse becomes the little rabbit's companion and helps him along in his new surroundings. One day the rabbit asks the Skin Horse, "What is real?"

The Skin Horse gives an explanation of the beauty of being loved as a toy, getting your hair rubbed off, becoming loose in the joints, and becoming shabby. He tells the rabbit it takes time, it is a process, and it doesn't happen to those who break easily or have to be carefully kept. He ends the conversation by telling the rabbit that when you are real, you don't mind being hurt because it is a part of a process.

Being real and transparent is the opposite of being secretive about who we really are. When Jesus came, he ministered on earth as a real person. He was who he said he was and never pretended to be any different. He was authentic in all he did and said, which is why the Pharisees hated him so. He didn't hide behind religious robes and flaunt his Godhood. He was genuine and it frightened and disgusted the religious leaders of the day.

Jesus was very serious in his interactions with the Pharisees. He spoke quite harshly to them. *The Message Bible* by Eugene Peterson puts Jesus' words this way:

Matthew 23:2-37

> Now Jesus turned to address his disciples, along with the crowd that had gathered with them. "The religion scholars and Pharisees are competent teachers in God's Law. You won't go wrong in following their teachings on Moses. But be careful about following them. They talk a good line, but they don't live it. They don't take it into their hearts and live it out in their behavior. It's all spit-and-polish veneer.

"Instead of giving you God's Law as food and drink by which you can banquet on God, they package it in bundles of rules, loading you down like pack animals. They seem to take pleasure in watching you stagger under these loads, and wouldn't think of lifting a finger to help. Their lives are perpetual fashion shows, embroidered prayer shawls one day and flowery prayers the next. They love to sit at the head table at church dinners, basking in the most prominent positions, preening in the radiance of public flattery, receiving honorary degrees, and getting called 'Doctor' and 'Reverend.'

"Don't let people do that to you, put you on a pedestal like that. You all have a single Teacher, and you are all classmates. Don't set people up as experts over your life, letting them tell you what to do. Save that authority for God; let him tell you what to do. No one else should carry the title of 'Father'; you have only one Father, and he's in heaven. And don't let people maneuver you into taking charge of them. There is only one Life-Leader for you and them—Christ.

"Do you want to stand out? Then step down. Be a servant. If you puff yourself up, you'll get the wind knocked out of you. But if you're content to simply be yourself, your life will count for plenty.

"Frauds!

"I've had it with you! You're hopeless, you religion scholars, you Pharisees! Frauds! Your lives are roadblocks to God's kingdom. You refuse to enter, and won't let anyone else in either.

"You're hopeless, you religion scholars and Pharisees! Frauds! You go halfway around the world to make a convert, but once you get him you make him into a replica of yourselves, double-damned.

"You're hopeless! What arrogant stupidity! You say, 'If someone makes a promise with his fingers crossed, that's nothing; but if he swears with his hand on the Bible, that's serious.' What ignorance! Does the leather on the Bible carry more weight than the skin on your hands? And what about this piece of trivia: 'If you shake hands on a promise, that's nothing; but if you raise your hand that God is your witness, that's serious'? What ridiculous hairsplitting! What difference does it make whether you shake hands or raise hands? A promise is a promise. What difference does it make if you make your promise inside or outside a house of worship? A promise is a promise. God is present, watching and holding you to account regardless.

"You're hopeless, you religion scholars and Pharisees! Frauds! You keep meticulous account books, tithing on every nickel and dime you get, but on the meat of God's Law, things like fairness and compassion and commitment—the absolute basics!—you carelessly take it or leave it. Careful bookkeeping is commendable, but the basics are required. Do you have any idea how silly you look, writing a life story that's wrong from start to finish, nitpicking over commas and semicolons?

"You're hopeless, you religion scholars and Pharisees! Frauds! You burnish the surface of your cups and bowls so they sparkle in the sun, while the insides are maggoty with your greed and gluttony. Stupid Pharisee! Scour the insides, and then the gleaming surface will mean something.

"You're hopeless, you religion scholars and Pharisees! Frauds! You're like manicured grave plots, grass clipped and the flowers bright, but six feet down it's all rotting bones and worm-eaten flesh. People look at you and think you're saints, but beneath the skin you're total frauds.

"You're hopeless, you religion scholars and Pharisees! Frauds! You build granite tombs for your prophets and marble monuments for your saints. And you say that if you had lived in the days of your ancestors, no blood would have been on your hands. You protest too much! You're cut from the same cloth as those murderers, and daily add to the death count.

"Snakes! Reptilian sneaks! Do you think you can worm your way out of this? Never have to pay the piper? It's on account of people like you that I send prophets and wise guides and scholars generation after generation—and generation after generation you treat them like dirt, greeting them with lynch mobs, hounding them with abuse.

"You can't squirm out of this: Every drop of righteous blood ever spilled on this earth, beginning with the blood of that good man Abel right down to the blood of Zechariah, Barachiah's son, whom you murdered at his prayers, is on your head. All this, I'm telling you, is coming down on you, on your generation.

"Jerusalem! Jerusalem! Murderer of prophets! Killer of the ones who brought you God's news! How often I've ached to embrace your children, the way a hen gathers her chicks under her wings, and you wouldn't let me. And now you're so desolate, nothing but a ghost town. What is there left to say? Only this: I'm out of here soon. The next time you see me you'll say, 'Oh, God has blessed him! He's come, bringing God's rule!'"

List your thoughts on what you have just read. How does it strike you? Do you think Jesus was being fair and honest with them? Why or why not?

DAY THREE

Now read this passage again in your own Bible—Matthew 23:2-37. Jesus lists eight woes. Record them next to the verses listed. (Note: The NIV and NLT translations have omitted verse 14.)

Woe 1 v. 13

Woe 2 v. 14

Woe 3 v. 15

Woe 4 v. 16

Woe 5 v. 23

Woe 6 v. 25

Woe 7 v. 27

Woe 8 v. 29

Jesus also calls them something else. Fill in the blanks next to the verses to find out what else he says about the Pharisees.

V. 17 blind_____

V. 19 blind_____

V. 24 blind_____

V. 26 blind_____

As we have read and learned, the Pharisees were fraudulent phonies. Jesus is very clear about what God thinks about this subject. How often have we read those words about the Pharisees only to miss the point given? We are just like them, with only a slight tweak for the twenty-first century Church. We hide our sin for fear of embarrassment; we lead others astray with pretenses of "togetherness." The motivation to put up masks or veils in this area can be many: rejection, fear of what others will think about us, etc. But the truth is, when we are authentic and transparent with each other, incredible unity is promoted and compassion to love in the body is experienced. Being authentic frees us up because we all are in the same position—imperfect people who need Jesus Christ to navigate through life!

What are you hiding from others right now? Talk to God about it and ask him to help you be more open in sharing the challenges you may be facing at this moment. If you are not facing anything right now, think about the last time you were really struggling. How did you handle your struggle? Make an effort this week to be honest when someone asks, "How are you?"

DAY FOUR

Secrecy's cousin is deception. Look up the following verses and see what the Scripture has to say about deceit and deception. Write what you learn from each verse.

Psalm 12:2

Psalm 52:2

Psalm 101:7

Proverbs 14:8

Proverbs 26:24

Jeremiah 9:6, 8

Hosea 10:13

2 Corinthians 4:2

1 Peter 2:1

Write out the blessing or promise that God gives in this verse: Psalm 32:2

Read 1 Peter 2:22. Whose example are we to follow?

The realization that we are being deceptive or deceitful when we are secretive or not altogether authentic is not a pleasant one. But according to what we find in God's Word, it is a reality. Putting on a façade or trying to be someone or something we are not is sin, and it is deceitful. This is rarely discussed in our churches and we somehow live with the illusion that we need to present ourselves without any flaws. How sad! I often wonder why people would even want to get next to us and come to our churches if we can't be real. Jesus came for the broken and that includes all of us!

In closing today, write out what God has revealed to you about your heart in this area. I encourage you to name it for what it is. He already knows and there is no fear of being unloved or rejected as we come to our loving heavenly Father.

Also, share it this week with someone you trust. Ask him or her to pray for you and with you. I pray that God will give you his unfathomable peace and sense of deep love as you allow him to help you in your areas of struggle.

DAY FIVE

This week has not been an easy one to study. It is always uncomfortable to confront our own sinful nature. As I was writing this lesson, God impressed me with something that I had been keeping from my husband, a mistake I had made that I needed to share with him. I wrestled and even tried to bargain with God. In his gentleness and mercy, the Spirit helped me to see that I needed to be up front and honest about it.

After days of agonizing and praying, I told Kevin. I was met with God's grace and forgiveness. God is so good! And I felt the burden of secrecy lifted. Our theme verse states … "as we turn to the Lord, the veil is taken away … and there is freedom!" Freedom results from obedience and turning or reversing the process of sin in our lives.

As you reflect on your life, is there anything you are hiding from someone or even from God? Make a commitment to deal with it this very moment so you can be released from the burden of carrying it.

This week I am going to leave you with two passages from Oswald Chambers's *My Utmost For His Highest*[1]. May you be deeply inspired as you read this man's insight and wisdom.

Reflection

What to renounce

"We have renounced the hidden things of shame … " (2 Corinthians 4:2). Have you "renounced the hidden things of shame" in your life—the things that your sense of honor or pride will not allow to come into the light? You can easily hide them. Is there a thought in your heart about anyone that you would not like to be brought into the light? Then renounce it as soon as it comes to mind—renounce everything in its entirety until there is no hidden dishonesty or craftiness about you at all.

Envy, jealousy, and strife don't necessarily arise from your old nature of sin, but from the flesh, which was used for these kinds of things in the past (see Romans 6:19 and 1 Peter 4:1-3). You must maintain continual watchfulness so that nothing arises in your life that would cause you shame.

"Not walking in craftiness … " (2 Corinthians 4:2). This means not resorting to something simply to make your own point. This is a terrible trap. You know that God will allow you to work successfully in only one way—the way of truth. Be careful never to catch people through the other way—the way of deceit. If you act deceitfully, God's blight and ruin will be upon you. What may be craftiness for you may not be for others—God has called you to a higher standard.

Never dull your sense of being your utmost for his highest—your best for his glory. For you, doing certain things would mean craftiness coming into your life for a purpose other than what is the highest and best, and it would dull the motivation that God has given you. Many people have turned back because they are afraid to look at things from God's perspective. The greatest spiritual crisis comes when a person has to move a little farther on in his faith than the beliefs he has already accepted."

Take notes on what you just read. What impresses you about these writings?

DARKNESS OR FREEDOM

AM I ANGRY?

DAY ONE

 several years ago I woke up to a beautiful sunny, snowy day. I was going through my morning routine of tea and devotions when I stepped into the living room. As I made my way to open the window shades, I noticed three blotches on our living room carpet! Immediately my spirit turned from joy of anticipating a great day to mumbling and grumbling while I cleaned up the mess from our dog Maggie. You see, Maggie likes to eat undesirables from the yard when she does her business and as a result almost always gets sick.

This morning she had not only gotten sick, but also decided to leave a nice deposit in the only room of the house in which she isn't allowed. So as I was scrubbing and cleaning the carpet, I sensed God's spirit speaking to me about my anger. Was I going to allow this flame of anger to ignite from a brush fire to an all out forest fire? Or was I going to apply what I had been learning?

There is a history of anger in my family that runs long and deep on both sides. It was most visible on my dad's side. Although I grew up in a very loving home, my dad often exhibited explosive anger with us, which sometimes took on the form of uncontrollable rage. In spite of my dad's anger, I have deep respect for him because he always came to us and asked our forgiveness, acknowledging his wrongdoing even though he was not a Christian. He was dealing with his ghosts from the past, rejection from his father and the alcoholism of his mother. More than anything, he wanted a loving and real family.

As a child I felt sorry for my dad, and yet I loved him so deeply for working so hard to create the family he never had. Today, my father is a godly man who is gentle and affectionate with his children and grandchildren. God has turned the pain of his past into an instrument of healing and grace for many people.

Having that kind of anger modeled for me, and being a strong-willed child myself, I opted to express anger like my dad did, with temper tantrums and the like. I just thought it was normal. As I grew older, my anger took on new shapes and forms. Becoming a Christian as a young teenager, I was led to believe that my anger was wrong. I tried very hard to control it myself. After all, Christians don't get angry do they? And if they do, they certainly shouldn't talk about it. So the harder I tried, the harder it was and occasionally I would have explosive outbursts like my father. All those years it was about me, my control, my struggles with anger.

When Kevin and I were married, I brought this and other baggage with me into our marriage. Because of other conflicts as a young married couple, the anger grew worse. When we moved to Seattle from California, I finally realized I couldn't change this alone and asked someone to help me address my anger. It has been a long process over the years, but God has been faithful to work his discipline and mercy on the journey.

I came to realize over the years that my anger was yet another veil that was clouding my mirror. Not only was it destructive to me, but also to my family and to the testimony of ministering in the kingdom.

Today I would like us to look at anger from God's perspective. Read Ephesians 4:26-32. What does this passage say about being angry?

Now read this passage again and in the columns below contrast what we are to do and not to do.

SINS WE ARE TO PUT OFF	VIRTUES WE ARE TO PUT ON

Why do you think all these other sins are listed when Paul talks about anger in this passage?

Now read Ephesians 4:17-24. What do verses 23 and 24 give as the remedy for casting off our sin?

You were taught, with regard to your former way of life, to put off your _____, which is being corrupted by its deceitful desires; to be made_____in the attitude of your _____; and to put on the _____, created to be like_____in true _____ and holiness.

To close today's lesson, write a summary of what you have learned about anger.

DAY TWO

As we learned from our study in Day One from Ephesians 4:26, God gives us permission to get angry. God created the emotion of anger. It is what we do with that emotion that makes it right or wrong. Let's look at the following passages and see what we can learn about God's anger in the Bible.

Psalm 103:8-9

Isaiah 12:1-2

Isaiah 54:8

Joel 2:12-13

Micah 7:18

According to these passages, how is God's anger different from our anger?

David is mentioned in Scripture as a "man after God's own heart." Even though he was a very godly and righteous king, he was still human and fell into temptation and sin. There is a story of such a time in David's leadership when he deliberately sinned against God in taking a census of the Israelites. The Lord specifically forbade this practice. Read the account of God's anger towards David and the consequences of his actions in 1 Chronicles 21:1-19.

Verse 7 says, "This command was also evil in the sight of God; so he punished Israel." Why do you think God was displeased with David for numbering Israel in a census?

What observations can you make about David and his relationship with God during this time?

How did God exercise his mercy in disciplining David for this sin?

I hope in today's lesson you have gotten a glimpse of the patience our loving Father as he deals with our anger. I know that my sin is deserving of his full wrath and punishment. I marvel over and over again at God's grace in my life when I have failed or disappointed him with my actions.

As we close today, think of a time recently when you experienced God's grace over sin in your life. Write a prayer of thanksgiving expressing your gratitude to Him.

DAY THREE

As I shared at the beginning of this lesson, I expressed my anger the way I had understood it from my family. Through the years as God helped root out my anger, one of my regrets has been the effect my anger had on my children when they were young. I have cried many tears and appealed to God not to allow my ugly actions of anger to harm them emotionally. As I have been faithful and obedient in this area of my life, it has created accountability within our family. We give each other permission to confront and help each other do the right thing.

My prayer is for anger in my family to be broken in this generation, that it would not be passed down, but rather healing and permission to grow would happen as a result. Now that our children are grown with families of their own, I am beginning to reap the blessing of the obedience of bringing my anger captive to Christ and the work of his Spirit. As I watch my sons and their wives parent their small kids, I marvel at the grace and patience God has given them and it astounds me.

Crossing the line and allowing our anger to turn into sin not only affects us, but also deeply affects those closest to us. The Bible lists the consequences and negative results of allowing our anger to turn into sin. Look up the following verses and note what happens when our anger takes hold.

Ecclesiasties 7:9

The result:

Proverbs 14:29

The result:

Proverbs 29:22

The result:

Ephesians 4:26

The result:

Reflect on the past week and remember the last time you got angry. What happened? Did your anger turn into sin? What was the negative result of the situation? Talk to the Lord about it. If you haven't already, ask his forgiveness and write it out in a prayer. God is so loving and patient with us. I wish I could undo many actions that my anger caused, but I rest in the promise from Philippians 1:6: "He who began a good work in *me* will be faithful to complete it" (my paraphrase).

Satan desires to keep us in a place of shame and bondage with our anger. God desires to help us rise above our sin and by his Spirit, nothing is impossible. Allow God to speak to you in this moment if you are in this battle with your anger. Lay down your weapons and surrender to allow God to do his work in releasing you.

It won't be easy; it will be three steps forward and two steps back some days. But God stands there waiting with open arms each time we surrender to his will and his ways. Take that step right now and tell him your need.

DAY FOUR

The topic of anger could easily be a whole Bible study in itself. There is so much to unpack once the anger veil is revealed and lifted. When God first spoke to me about my anger, I was overwhelmed with the enormity of how great a stronghold it had become in my life. Looking back, I am so grateful that he took me one step at a time to deal with it.

The lesson this week is just a small step in that direction. If you struggle with anger, I would encourage you to explore some further steps. You may need to seek out a godly counselor or join a recovery group as God leads you. There are many great resources available, for which I am grateful.

One of the best resources, of course, is the Bible. Today we are going to explore the positive results that come from keeping our anger under control.

Look up the following verses and note the results.

Psalm 4:4

Proverbs 15:1

Proverbs 29:8, 11

James 1:19-20

As much as anger comes out in our behavior, an equal amount is displayed through our actions, but one of the most deadly ways anger gets out of control is because of our tongue. Remember the saying, "Sticks and stones may break my bones, but words will never hurt me"? This lie we inwardly chanted as children while insults were hurled at us mask deeply wounded hearts at times.

Read James 3:1-12. List those things to which James compares the tongue.

Make a list of the six things of which the tongue is capable:

1.

2.

3.

4.

5.

6.

Name a time recently when you allowed your tongue to get out of control. What were the circumstances? What could you have done differently?

Take one of the verses that spoke to you today and write it out on a 3 x 5 card and put it up in a place that will remind you of what you have learned in preventing your anger from getting out of control.

DAY FIVE

The veil of anger seems to cloak and shroud many in our culture today. We see it in the form of road rage, domestic violence, bullying in our schools, random shootings, discontent in our places of work and sadly, yes, even in our churches. Our world is angry and many people don't even know from where their anger comes. Anger is a deadly poison when it takes its victim and can lead to bitterness, unforgiveness, and deep woundedness. It would be impossible in today's lesson to address all of these things, but I would like to address the immense importance of forgiveness as it relates to anger.

We have mostly examined anger when it's out of control and affecting others. But what happens when we have been affected by another person's anger or have been deeply wounded or hurt? Our anger may or may not be justified, but forgiveness is needed for personal wholeness.

I would like to suggest three keys to finding freedom in forgiveness.
Before we begin to unlock these keys, let's look at the story of Joseph.

Read:

Genesis 37:3-4, 18-36

Genesis 39:1-23

Genesis 41:14-44

Genesis 42:1-11

Looking at the life of Joseph and his dilemma, the keys are:

Key One - Face the hurt

Joseph was certainly a target of his brothers' jealousy and envy. How could he forgive them? Read what the brothers were discussing in Genesis 42:21-24. How did Joseph react?

Key Two - Grieve the loss

Grieving is part of the process of facing what is real. It is part of the necessary preparation of forgiveness. Read in Genesis 43:26-31 Joseph's reaction to the long separation of his family. What prompted Joseph to leave the room hastily?

Key Three - Letting go

Letting go is a very important part of the forgiveness process. We may not be able to forget, but we can let go to halt the creeping in of bitterness. Read in Genesis 45:1-15 what happens to Joseph when he comes to terms with his brothers.

In forgiving his brothers, what were some of the benefits of freedom that Joseph experienced?

This was a difficult lesson to study and a challenge for me to write. I am not proud of my anger, and yet in sharing my challenges with you and others, I know we can encourage each other. The enemy wants us to believe that we are alone on our journey and wants to keep us bound up in our sins. But what a huge blessing it is that God designed us as relational beings to draw us together in our time of need. We need to pray for each other in this area and we need to allow the freedom to talk about our shortcomings within the church. We need to create a safe place to find forgiveness and healing as we grow together.

My prayer for you this week is that as God has revealed himself to you, he will give you his peace and rest to carry this struggle. God is good and rewards those who are faithful to be obedient to his Word. May his Spirit give you the power and the strength for the journey, and may you find freedom as the veil of anger is lifted!

Reflection

In your anger do not sin. Do not let the sun go down while you are still angry, and do not give the devil a foothold. Do not let any unwholesome talk come out of your mouths, but only what is helpful for building others up according to their needs, that it may benefit those who listen. And do not grieve the Holy Spirit of God, with whom you were sealed for the day of redemption. Get rid of all bitterness, rage and anger, brawling and slander, along with every form of malice. Be kind and compassionate to one another, forgiving each other just as in Christ God forgave you (Ephesians 4:26-27, 29-32).

DARKNESS OR FREEDOM

WHY DO I FEEL THIS WAY?

DAY ONE

I boarded a plane for Southern California feeling angry, frustrated, and confused. My dear friend and mother-in-law lay in a hospital bed, the shadow of death hovering. As I sat on the plane numb and expressionless, I cried out to God, "Lord, where are you?" She was one of few women in my life I felt safe with and I wasn't ready to lose her. Two weeks earlier, we had buried the spiritual rock of our family, my grandfather. I had the privilege of caring for and walking with him through his last days. And now mere weeks after his death and possibly facing another, I felt as though the foundation of my childhood had been bulldozed.

I was emotionally spent and I wanted to scream instead of cry, "Lord, I can't do this anymore!" I felt as though his face was shrouded from me.

This was one of the few times in my journey with God I truly felt that I had been abandoned by him.

This part of the journey had begun earlier that spring. I was diagnosed with clinical depression. The long days and weeks of caregiving had taken their toll. The blackness and despair sought to submerge me. *Depression*—that verdict was difficult to digest. I could swallow a diagnosis of arthritis, high blood pressure, or? But depression? In my mind depression was for weak people and weak Christians who didn't have enough faith. I argued with God, my counselor, pastor, and doctor, who were all trying to help me. I was a visible leader, a pastor's wife. What would people whisper about me behind closed doors if they knew? The lies flooded my mind.

At the outset of this dark season, I discovered that the depression wasn't just from the losses I had experienced during the past several months or my physical exhaustion; it was from deeper issues that had been tucked away for years. Issues of expectations and a warped perspective of needing to perform to be loved. And God began to bring them to the surface for me to address.

These lies were destroying me and had plunged my spiritual and emotional being into the dark hole of depression. Performance had a stronghold in my heart, life, and ministry that God in his faithfulness desired to root out of me. My depression was a symptom of something deeper, something I needed to face in order to be a whole person. Something I needed to do so that I could look to reflect God's glory in my life in a more effective way.

Depression is on the rise in our culture and in a recent webinar, I heard Leslie Vernick, counselor and coach, share in her talk about depression that the World Health Organization predicts that by the year 2030 depression will be the second largest disability for women behind HIV and AIDS. Thirty percent of those who suffer from depression are women.

Depressed Christians often experience an added spiritual struggle that complicates depression. The Church is only beginning to acknowledge the sober reality of depression instead of seeing it as a sign of weakness or spiritual failure. Many Christians who experience depression do so alone because of their fear of rejection or being told that their faith is weak.

My good friend and counselor used this illustration. If I had a broken leg, would I lie on the couch, not tell anyone, and just hope it would heal? No! I would go to the doctor immediately to get treatment. The same must be true for depression; a person often needs treatment medically to overcome their extreme feelings of despair and hopelessness. It is only then that they will be able to explore the root of what is causing the depression so it doesn't lead to a lifetime of chronic despair.

Depression veils hundreds of women in the church each year. I believe it is our responsibility to help women walk through this time with prayer, encouragement, and hope that "this too shall pass." The Bible shows that depression is very real through the life stories of Job, David, Elijah, and many others who struggled with it. This week we are going on a journey through the pages of the Bible to look at God's people who struggled with depression.

My prayer this week is for you to be encouraged if you are struggling with this veil. Before we begin, I want to give a disclaimer. I do not in any way presume to be an expert in this area. Depression is caused by many things and can be quite complicated. I am sharing out of my own experience in hopes that it will reveal the need for support in the body of Christ. If you or someone you know is struggling, I would strongly suggest they visit their doctor and speak to a qualified counselor.

To begin this week, we are going to read the story of Elijah. Find a quiet place so that you can immerse yourself in this story. As you read, envision the places, the sights, and the smells of what is happening in the story. Before you begin, ask the Holy Spirit to reveal the power of this story to you. So often we read it as "just a story." Today, read it as a testimony of one of God's children.

Elijah - Depression resulting from fatigue and exhaustion

Read 1 Kings 18. What was happening under King Ahab's leadership during this time of history?

Make a list of all the that Elijah did for God in this chapter:

Describe what happened on Mount Carmel:

Read 1 Kings 19:1-9. Why did Queen Jezebel want Elijah dead?

What was Elijah's response?

Contrast the Elijah of chapter 18 vs. the Elijah of chapter 19. What do you see?

Verse four says Elijah prayed that *he might die.* Is this the same Elijah who had such victory on Mt. Carmel? We can draw the conclusion that much of the reason he felt the way he did was due to utter exhaustion from the previous events. He needed rest and renewal. Look in verses 5-8. How did the Lord meet his need in response to his prayer?

Think back over the last few weeks or months. When was the last time you felt like Elijah under the broom tree? What were the circumstances?

When we are burned out, weary, and tired, it's easy to lose perspective. Sometimes the best thing we can do is sleep! I love this passage because of the way it says that God took care of Elijah. He met his needs right where he was. He needed the basics—a good meal and some sleep! Depression can creep in unnoticed if we don't take the time to take care of the basics. In closing today, write out what restores you when you are exhausted and weary.

DAY TWO

David - Depression resulting from outside circumstances

Read 1 Samuel 23:13-29. Name some of the emotions David must have felt while in hiding.

How did God protect David?

Who did God send to encourage David (verses 17-18)? Describe their relationship.

When was the last time you were in hiding because of outward circumstances? How did you feel? How did God bring you through?

Psalm 17 is a prayer David may have written while in hiding. Read this psalm and make a list of all the things David is asking God to do for him.

Taking the list you just made, write it as a prayer for yourself for what you might be facing right now. Commit it to the Lord and speak to him about your needs.

DAY THREE

Jonah - Depression resulting from disobedience

Sometimes whether we want to admit it or not, we can be led into depression by our own choices—choices of blatant sin and disobedience. Ouch! A harsh reality, but true. Admittedly, there have been times in my life when God has asked me to do something and I have chosen disobedience. Consequences and depression have followed until I surrendered to the Lord once again. In the deception of the sin, it may take a while for God to get our attention and for us to realize we have grieved the Holy Spirit with our actions. Jonah is a clear illustration of someone who sidestepped what God had asked. His consequences were severe, but God knows what will bring each of us to the place of surrender!

When Kevin and I were called to minister in Canada, it was a sheer step of obedience. It wasn't our choice, but God made it so clear to us we could not ignore the call to come. I can remember having many doubts and wasn't sure God knew what he was asking of us.

He led me to the story of Jonah, and I was reminded that to surrender in obedience was better than ending up in the belly of a whale, whatever that might have looked like in the twenty-first century! It wasn't easy and we wrestled with it, but peace and joy came as we took the first steps of obedience.

Now, years later, we've come full circle and are back home and God has made it possible to continue to minister in Canada and yet live close to our families on the other side of the border. I like to say we have one foot in each country!

Read Jonah 1 and 2. What was God asking Jonah to do?

Why do you think he was so reluctant?

How did the sailors respond to their passenger when the storm arose?

Describe the emotions Jonah must have felt after being swallowed by the whale.

Paraphrase Jonah's prayer from the belly of the whale in chapter two.

What do you think motivated Jonah to change his mind?

Describe a time in your life recently when you responded to God the way Jonah did? What were the circumstances? How did you respond? What did you learn?

DAY FOUR

Hannah - Depression resulting from loss

Depression can be a result of deep sorrow and grief. It can cause a myriad of symptoms as our bodies react to the loss. There may be disturbed sleep, loss of appetite, pervading fatigue, crying more than usual, or extreme feelings of sadness and hopelessness, to name a few.

During the darkest days of my depression, there were profound feelings of hopelessness. At times I would fear for my family—would I ever get well? It was hard to do even simple tasks. I had isolated myself from most of life and allowed only a few trusted and safe people in. The series of losses I had experienced over such a short period of time had plunged my body, spirit, and soul into darkness.

I cried out desperately to the Lord, asking him to remind me of his love daily, for he seemed miles away. God was so good to me during that time; he was faithful to remind me of his never-ending love. He whispered to me of his peace and healing through cards, a song, flowers one day that arrived on my doorstep with the note "to remind you today of God's great love," and many other ways.

Hannah, in 1 Samuel, had a significant heartache. Her childless state was mercilessly taunted by her husband's other wife. Cruel words and reminders of her pain caused her to sink in despair. Read her story in 1 Samuel 1.

What was the loss that Hannah was feeling? Why was she so sad?

Why do you think Peninnah treated Hannah the way she did?

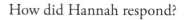

How did Hannah respond?

Describe what happened in the temple as she went to pray.

What was the promise that Hannah made?

How do you think could she make such a promise?

First Samuel, chapter two is Hannah's response to God answering her prayer. As you read through the prayer, list the attributes she names about God.

Verse 11 says that Hannah returns home with her husband without Samuel. Describe what you think her emotions might have been.

The Bible doesn't say how many years it was before Hannah had Samuel. The beginning of the book indicates that it might have been several years. She was grieved to the point of not eating and possibly other physical symptoms as well. Her sorrow was made worse by her home life and the continued pettiness and taunting of Peninnah. Despite her circumstances, she continued to wait on the Lord and draw her strength from him.

Have you ever had a Hannah experience? Maybe you are in the midst of such a situation right now. Write a prayer expressing your heart. You can be confident that the God who created you hears your prayer!

DAY FIVE

Juanita Ryan, in her article "Listening to Depression," says this:

Depression comes to us with a message. Depression signals to us that something has happened or is threatening to happen that touches a very deep part of who we are. Depression is like an alarm system calling us to pay attention .... When we are depressed we need to recognize that we are depressed, we need to give ourselves a break, we need to stay as engaged as possible, and we need to explore the meaning of the loss or the potential loss that faces us."[2]

The following verses are great words of comfort and hope. Read the verses and then make a note of how God's promises comfort those who are distressed or in despair.

Psalm 34:18

Psalm 91:14-15

Jeremiah 29:11

---

[2] Article taken from http://www.nacr.org/wordpress/120/listening-to-depression. Juanita Ryan is a therapist in private practice at Brea Family Counseling Center, Brea, California.

Lamentations 3:21-26

Isaiah 46:4

Ezekial 34:11-12

As we close today, my prayer is that you have seen from the truth in God's Word that our hope is in him and him alone. Depression is a difficult package to unwrap and as valuable as that time was in my own life, I pray I never have to return to that place of darkness.

Yet I know that because of that time, my relationship with my Lord and Savior is forever changed. He is my rock and my refuge even when my mind, heart, and emotions tell me differently. He rescued me and helped me to once again see the rainbow. I have a deeper appreciation for those who suffer, waiting to recover and heal. Comfort, encouragement, and love are what we need to extend to those in our church to help them walk the journey of their own healing.

A critical thing to remember while recovering from depression is that we cannot do it alone. We need each other—we need God and other people who will love and support us during this time. People who struggle with depression can't often see the rainbow after the storm. It feels like they will never be the same, and they have forgotten what it is like to be normal again. In short, they need hope.

To end this week, I would like to encourage you to write a note of comfort to someone who might be struggling in this area. Keep it simple and brief, reminding them of your support to them. If you are the person who is suffering, I would encourage you to call someone you can trust and ask them to pray and walk the journey with you. Do what is necessary to begin the road of recovery.

Reflection

I cried out to the Lord in my suffering, and he heard me. He set me free from all my fears. For the angel of the Lord guards all who fear him, and he rescues them (Psalm 34:6-7).

PART III

Results of Removing the Veil

FREEDOM TO WORSHIP

DAY ONE

 go right now to your favorite coffee place and get the largest size latte of your choice or whatever your favorite might be. When I've worked hard, I like to think it's okay to reward myself, just saying!

I am so very proud of how hard you have worked these past six weeks on your study. I know that looking at your soul mirror in depth, lifting the veils of performance, anger, secrecy, and depression was not easy. It probably felt like an uphill climb, clawing and scratching to keep your balance.

Thank you for letting me meddle and be your guide. I hope and pray this week you will begin to sense the freedom that is just around the corner.

When our children were in elementary school and junior high, we had the privilege of traveling overseas and visiting eleven countries. While in Germany, we met a family who took us to the former East-West border. It had been a mere six years since the Berlin Wall and the Iron Curtain had come down, and what we saw impressed us deeply. The woman took us down a country road to the former border and we stopped to get out of the car. She pointed to the deep ruts in the road created by military tanks where the barbed wire had separated the two countries. We stood at the now-invisible barrier and looked first at the West and then to the East. To the West were well-kept homes with immaculate gardens and lots of color and life. When we looked past the ruts to the East, we saw gray—drab houses running down gray streets in gray villages.

She further explained to us that when the wall came down, those from the West brought large bunches of bananas to share with those from the Eastern bloc. "Bananas?" we asked, incredulous.

"Yes, bananas," was her profound reply. The communist leadership had determined which villages would grow what kind of produce, and since the communists viewed bananas as an unprofitable crop, people living in the East who once enjoyed bananas no longer had access to buy them.

Thus, when the wall came down they cried out, "Bring us bananas!" And so the Westerners did, and there was a celebration of bananas! Without their freedom they were not allowed to enjoy life to the fullest. The communist leaders had dictated to them where they would work, what they would eat, where they could travel, what they should wear, and how they should live. To our American minds, this was unfathomable oppression. My children had a greater appreciation for bananas after that.

Freedom is a wonderful thing. The tapestry of history is interwoven with stories of freedom and the cost of sacrifices men and women have made for freedom. Freedom simply means: the quality or state of being free, such as the absence of necessity, coercion, or constraint in choice or action; liberation from slavery or restraint or from the power of the quality or state of being exempt or released usually from something onerous (www.merriam-webster.com/dictionary/freedom).

Christians have the opportunity to live eternally in freedom because of the sacrifice of God's Son Jesus Christ. He died so we could be free—free from the bondage of sin, free from the veils that would cover our hearts and lives preventing us from reflecting his image.

I want us to look again at 2 Corinthians 3:16-18.

But whenever anyone turns to the Lord, the veil is taken away. Now the Lord is the Spirit, and where the Spirit of the Lord is, there is freedom. [18]And we, who with unveiled faces all reflect the Lord's glory, are being transformed into his likeness with ever-increasing glory, which comes from the Lord, who is the Spirit.

Again, this passage reminds us that the veil is taken away when we *turn to the Lord*. And when we do, God's Spirit is there and freedom is the result! Today we are going to explore the word *freedom* from Scripture as it relates to our study. Then we will uncover the treasures that come from being free in Christ.

Read John 8:31-36. What does Jesus say are the keys to freedom in this passage?

Read the following verses and make note of how the Bible describes freedom and what is required to obtain freedom in Christ Jesus.

Psalm 119:45

Isaiah 61:1

Luke 4:18

Romans 5:6-8

Ephesians 3:12

James 1:25

How do the following Scriptures warn about abusing our freedom?

1 Peter 2:16

Galatians 5:13

What are some ways that Christians and the Church have abused freedom in Christ?

According to Scripture, our freedom comes with responsibility. When we walk in the truth of God's Word, the freedom that Christ gives brings reward and blessing to our lives. To close today, write down what you have learned about your freedom in Christ. Maybe there is a need to confess ways that you have misused your freedom and now that freedom has become like bondage to you. Talk to the Lord about it and surrender to Him once again.

DAY TWO

Experiencing freedom in Christ without our veils brings many benefits. One of those benefits is the freedom to worship. Don't mistake me for only meaning corporate worship on Sunday mornings. I am speaking about our worship as a verb. *Worship is a consuming desire to give to God and involves the giving of our heart attitudes, our possessions, and ourselves.* Worship is to be our lifestyle in everything we do, from the time we get up in the morning to the time our head hits the pillow at night. When we live an unveiled life, worship becomes a part of our whole being, actions, and attitudes; and what follows is tremendous freedom.

Read the following in Psalms and note what the psalmist says about worship:

Psalm 29:2

Psalm 86:9

Psalm 95:6

Psalm 99:5, 9

Psalm 100:2

What theme do you see running through these verses?

DAY THREE

The life of Daniel is an example of a man who lived his whole life as an act of worship before the Lord. God gave Daniel favor with the kings he served under during his lifetime. He was put to the test during the reign of King Darius. Read the account in Daniel chapter 6.

What unique gifts and abilities had God given Daniel (Daniel 1:17)?

Why do you think the others were searching to find fault in Daniel? Be specific.

What action did Daniel take after the decree was signed (verse 10)?

What do you think gave Daniel the freedom to worship?

How did God provide a way of escape? What was the result in the kingdom?

Give an explanation of what you think Daniel's relationship with God was like? Why?

This is a powerful account of Daniel's trust in and faithfulness to God and his Word. Write a prayer that expresses your desire to live a life of worship in the midst of our present day Babylon.

DAY FOUR

The temptation to worship something/someone other than God with our lives is a great danger.

God is very specific in his Word about worshipping anything other than him; he takes it very seriously. God especially despises our token worship when we have lived lives apart from him. Read the account of Judah's people in Jeremiah 7:1-29. Make note of the lifestyle of the people of Judah. Make a list of what was keeping them from truly worshipping God.

Why couldn't God accept their worship? What did he desire most from them?

Where are you right now in regard to your worship before the Lord? Are you participating in corporate worship only as token act, or are you experiencing worship freely by acknowledging and recognizing your need for surrender in every area of your life? Take an honest inventory and write out your thoughts. This is between you and God; he knows the deepest places of your heart and longs to have you worship him in spirit and in truth.

DAY FIVE

The Psalms express the heart of one who desires to worship and praise God wholeheartedly. King David, who penned many of these psalms, was called *a man after God's own heart*—a man who truly had an intimate relationship with God.

One only has to read the book of Psalms to understand that David shared his deepest sorrows and ecstasies of joy with his Creator. He held back nothing and we learn much, not only about his life, but also about the many emotions he wrestled with during his lifetime. One of the most beautiful pictures of King David's incredible love for God was written shortly after he became the rightful king of Israel. Read the account of David when he returns the ark of the covenant to Jerusalem in 2 Samuel 6:12-23.

How did David celebrate the return of the ark of the covenant? List in order the events that happened.

What was David's wife, Michal's, response? Why do you think she was so disgusted?

Read in 2 Samuel 7:1-16 God's response to David's expression of worship and his heart in ruling the kingdom. What did God promise?

Read David's prayer of thanks in verses 18-29 of 2 Samuel 7. Being free to worship comes as a result of living a surrendered life. David lived authentically and openly before the Father and as a result was free to worship as God created him. His prayers express what we cannot articulate at times.

In closing this week, reread David's prayer. Paraphrase it to reflect your own thankfulness and worship to God for what he has done for you and his sovereignty over your life.

Reflection

I will walk about in freedom, for I have sought out your precepts (Psalm 119:45).

FREEDOM TO LOVE OTHERS

DAY ONE

One of the joys of living an unveiled life is the freedom to genuinely love others. When our own veils are removed and we stand confident in Christ, we are then able to see people as God sees them. We are less judgmental, or we sooner recognize the temptation to judge. We learn to appreciate the diversity of the body because we understand the truth of what God's Word says about the body of Christ and the need we have for all parts to function together. We are more likely to have understanding in difficult situations. We experience freedom in loving others because we are aware of our own struggle to remain unveiled.

Picture with me for a moment a lovely young bride walking slowly, lightly, down the aisle toward her beloved groom. She wears a veil borne of tradition to symbolize her virginity, her purity. During the ceremony the groom is allowed to lift the veil and kiss her, symbolizing his acceptance of her. But what happens to the bride's literal vision when the veil is lifted? She can see her groom clearly, and he can see her. What does she see? She sees the fine details of her beloved—his eyelashes and subtle color variations in his eyes; the curve of his chin, razor stubbled; the funny cowlick at the right side of his forehead. He sees the lips he can hardly wait to kiss, her cheekbones lightly rouged, the blemish she desperately tried to cover over for this special day, the smeared mascara brought about by her tears of joy.

Oh, yes, the unveiled life is glorious because we are free to see the Lord's glory in its fullest. And we are free to stand before the Lord with all our flaws, completely accepted and loved. But no less important is the fact that though we are free to see the flaws and blemishes of others, we accept and love them completely with grace, just as we have been accepted with grace.

Having the freedom to love others the way God intended us to sends a powerful message of acceptance within the church and to our communities.

Read the following passages and note what God says about genuine love.

1 John 3:11-19

1 John 4:7-21

2 John v. 5-6

Loving others is a not an optional virtue. We are commanded to love. John even goes so far as to say we are liars if we claim to love God but fail to love those whom he created. But you and I both know loving our fellow human beings isn't easy, sometimes not even desirable. In fact, the hardest part of loving is offering forgiveness to those who have wounded us. Worse yet, when we have acted in obedience and offered forgiveness, restoration of the relationship is not always the outcome. But God's Word gives us hope and gives us principles to live by and love by even in the darkest of circumstances.

"Therefore *encourage* one another and *build each other up*, just as in fact you are doing" (1 Thessalonians 5:11, emphasis added).

This week we are going to look at what it takes to encourage and build each other up in the context of love. The acrostic below lists five ways we will explore being free to love one another.

B   Bear with one another

U   Understand each other

I   Imitate Christ to each other

L   Listen and learn from each other

D   Discern the needs of each other

Bear with one another

The following passages give us prerequisites for bearing with one another. List them below:

Ephesians 4:1-3

Romans 15:1

Colossians 3:12-15

Think of the last time that you were hurt or offended by someone. What happened? Did you apply these principles? Write out what you could have done differently, if anything.

DAY TWO

Understand each other

Look at the following verses and note what precedes understanding.

Proverbs 2:2-3

Proverbs 4:5-7

Proverbs 9:10

Proverbs 23:23

Look at the following verses and note what God says about those who despise understanding.

Proverbs 18:2

Proverbs 21:16

Isaiah 6:10

Ephesians 4:18

There are both benefits to understanding and consequences. Look up the following verses and fill in the chart.

Proverbs 3:5-6, 13   Proverbs 16:22

Proverbs 10:23   Proverbs 19:8

Proverbs 11:12   Proverbs 24:3

Proverbs 13:15   Psalm 111:10

Proverbs 14:29   Proverbs 15:21

Proverbs 17:27   Proverbs 20:5

BENEFITS	CONSEQUENCES

Think about your relationships for a moment. Is there someone in your life to whom you need to give more understanding? Write out what you can do to love them in understanding.

DAY THREE

Imitate Christ to each other

Read Philippians 2:1-11. Make a list of all the qualities we are to have in our relationships.

Looking over the above list, name the relationship you have the most challenges with. Which of the qualities listed do you need help with? Why?

Look up the following verses and fill in on the drawing the six things we are to clothe ourselves with in our relationships.

Clothe yourself with ...
Colossians 3:12-15

State what Paul says in these Scriptures about forgiving others.

Whom do you need to approach with humility and exercise forgiveness? Write it out in a prayer to the Lord expressing your desire to restore and love this person.

DAY FOUR

Listen and learn from each other

What do these verses say about listening?

Proverbs 1:5

Proverbs 19:20

What is David asking in these verses?

Psalm 10:17

Psalm 17:1

Psalm 39:12

Psalm 54:2

Psalm 55:1

Psalm 86:6

Psalm 142:6

Psalm 143:1

What is the theme running through these verses?

We all have a desire to have people know and understand us. Each one of us values people who truly listen when we speak, especially when we are sharing our deepest thoughts. People who listen are safe people. Listening with understanding is so critical for a relationship to grow.

Note what Proverbs 18:13 says: "To answer before listening—that is folly and shame."

Read the account of Mary and Martha in Luke 10:38-42. What needs to happen to us before we can listen?

What are some steps we can take in order to be better listeners?

Over the next few days, be aware of your listening skills. Write down what you will do differently in order to listen more carefully.

DAY FIVE

Discern needs of each other

The following verses list the companions of discernment. Paraphrase each companion noted in the verse.

Proverbs 10:13

Proverbs 14:6

Proverbs 14:33

Proverbs 16:21

Proverbs 18:15

What do these verses say about a fool?

Proverbs 15:14

Proverbs 17:24

Read the account of Solomon in 1 Kings 3:5-14. What did the Lord promise to give to Solomon as a result of his request?

What was God asking of Solomon as a result?

Write why you think Solomon requested discernment above everything else?

Psalm 119:25 and Proverbs 3:21 are requests for discernment. Read these verses and then write them out as a personal prayer to God. Take some time to pray this prayer in regard to a relationship with which you need help.

When we experience freedom to love one another without our veils hindering or distracting us, we gain the ability to love and see others as God sees them. As we close this week, review the five characteristics of freedom to love others that we have studied this week from 1 Thessalonians 5:11. Now choose one of these that you would like to focus on in helping you to love others more effectively.

B -

U -

I -

L -

D -

Reflection

The wise in heart are called discerning, and pleasant words promote instruction (Proverbs 16:21).

FREEDOM TO TELL YOUR STORY

DAY ONE

Sitting across the table from me was a woman in her thirties who appeared much older. She had lived a hard life laced with broken relationships, drugs, and alcohol. As she spilled out her story of abuse and hurt, I was overwhelmed with compassion. Weeks earlier in a class for seekers, I had mistaken her as cold, hard, and unresponsive to the gospel. She seemed to avoid me at all costs, unwilling to make eye contact and moving to the opposite side of the room when I approached her.

I had been praying weeks before for those people in my life to whom I felt God wanted me to reach out. I sensed God speaking to me about learning to see others as he sees them. So when prompted, I asked Michelle out for coffee and even though she couldn't bring herself to look me in the eye, she accepted. Later, driving away from the first of what was to be many encounters with her, I was choked with emotion as I realized how much she needed God's love and forgiveness. I began to pray for more opportunities to show her God's love and share with her the good news.

One of the effects of coming out from the behind the veil is that the Holy Spirit gives us "God-vision" to see those around us the way he sees them, and to recognize and feel their pain. It would be easier to close our eyes and stop our ears in the face of overwhelming needs. And it is certainly easier to walk on by and pretend we don't see the hurt. The walls of our churches are deceptively safe. But God calls us to be witnesses for him—how do we do this? And what about sharing God's love with those who seem to have it all together with no apparent need?

Undeniably, the most effective tool in sharing the gospel is freedom. The freedom to love others is an irresistible aroma. When walking in freedom, people are more inclined to journey with you because the power of the Holy Spirit in your life is palpable. The first step of courage is to strip off the veils. Since courage breeds courage, we are then more quick to love people who don't know Jesus Christ whether they are hurt, lonely, or give the appearance of not needing anything at all. We become as 2 Corinthians 2:14-16 says a "life-giving perfume" (NLT). Who can resist the fragrance of love freely given?

Read Mark 16:15. What command does Jesus give to us?

Paraphrase these verses to apply to the twenty-first century.

Give your definition of what the "good news" is. Be specific and use at least two Scriptures. You may want to use a concordance to assist you in your answer.

According to these verses, how can you apply it to "your world"?

DAY TWO

Luke 4:18-19 and Luke 7:21-23 describe Jesus' mission. What had God called him to do? How was he able to accomplish it?

Isaiah 61:1-3 is the passage that Jesus read in the synagogue. Just as Jesus was anointed by the Father to bring the good news, by his Spirit we too can proclaim that news. What an awesome truth! It isn't up to us and our own methods, but because of God's Spirit within, that he anoints us to be the messengers of love to a lost and dying world. Read this passage in Isaiah and list the nine ways we are able to proclaim the good news of Jesus Christ.

The Spirit of the Sovereign Lord is on me, because the Lord has anointed me to:

1. _____ good news to the _____.

2. He has sent me to _____ up the _____,

3. To proclaim _____ for the _____

4. And _____ for the prisoners,

5. To _____ the year of the Lord's favor and the day of vengeance

of our God,

6. To _____ all who _____, and _____ for those

who grieve in Zion—

7. To bestow on them a _____ of _____instead of ashes, the

oil of gladness instead of mourning,

8. And a _____ of _____ instead of a _____

of _____. They will be called oaks of righteousness, a planting of the Lord

9. For the _____ of his _____.

Applying the verses in Isaiah, how can we become effective in spreading the good news? List some practical ways.

Think about the people God has placed in your life: at school, work, and in your community. Focus on three of those people you can influence for the kingdom. What are some ways you can begin or continue to share the good news with them? Be specific.

DAY THREE

One of the primary keys to effectiveness in sharing the good news is prayer. Many times as I have prayed, God has revealed to me ways to encourage and reach others in my life. Often in prayer, God will lead me to a specific idea or tangible way to minister his love.

This happened on one occasion in the summer when I was home by myself for a few days. I was feeling lonely and missing my family. Kevin and I had been praying for several of our neighbors and we were trying to keep in contact with them as often as we could. One of our neighbors had been feeling stressed from work. So as I was praying for them that morning, God gave me the idea to love them by making a special meal for them. I called them up and told them that I was going to bring them a surprise on Saturday evening. They resisted, but I insisted.

As I shopped and planned for this special meal, my loneliness disappeared. Saturday arrived and as I was preparing, I was humming and enjoying the warm summer day as I cooked in the kitchen. I gathered my best china, napkins, and serving dishes, loaded everything up, and delivered my surprise. They fussed and said that I shouldn't be doing this as I set the table with flowers, candles, and dishes. I lit the candles and then served them. I told them I would return in an hour to retrieve the dirty dishes. As my neighbor walked me to the door, she had tears in her eyes and said that no one ever had done anything like this before. I was shocked because here was a couple that often exhibited generous hospitality.

I went home truly blessed knowing that God had specifically directed me to love them in a unique way that was a great blessing to them. I told them that as I was praying for them in their stress of the week, God had led me to make them dinner. I am continually amazed that as God leads, others are blessed and have often needed that moment of encouragement. This happened not because of me, but because as I prayed, the Spirit prompted me to act with a gift of kindness.

Read 2 Corinthians 4:3-6. Name the reasons why it is important to pray for those to whom we are reaching out.

In closing today, take some time to pray for those in your life who need encouragement and to know that Jesus loves them.

DAY FOUR

In week two of our study, you were given the opportunity to write out your story. Sharing your faith with others effectively means being able to communicate the difference Jesus has made in your life. Most of the time, the best way to share your story is in short two- to three-minute segments. This gives the hearer a chance to get a "Readers Digest" version, so to speak, and then at another opportunity we may share more. Take your story that you have written out and answer the following:

Describe the events leading up to you receiving Christ.

Describe what happened when you made the commitment to follow Christ. List any verses, if any, that impacted you.

Describe what your life has been like since.

DAY FIVE

Today we are going to finish up your story. Using the answers from yesterday, write out your story. Use the following guidelines as you write:

- Begin by praying that God would help you to craft your life story in such a way that it could be used in the most effective way. Ask him to remind you of the details that need to be included and to release you from those you can leave out.

- Be authentic: Describe your thoughts and feelings.

- Be honest: Tell it like it really is.

Be careful to use phrases and words that a seeker can understand, and avoid using Christianese (i.e., words like redemption, sanctification, salvation—unless you are going to explain them).

When you're finished, ask someone you trust to read it and give you some feedback. Read it a second time after the feedback and make any changes, if necessary.

Being comfortable with sharing your story is key to being able to communicate the gospel effectively. There is a specific purpose for your life circumstances and the way you came to Christ. God has strategically placed you where you are so that you can be a light in the darkness. Your story is important! What God has done for you is your testimony of the good news of Jesus Christ. Being free to share that story is the gift that God entrusts to you.

I am amazed to know that God trusts me with his message and it is up to you and me to convey the truth so that others can be set free! I pray that you will be encouraged as God gives you opportunities to share your story with others. When our veils are gone, we are free to share authentically what Jesus has done for us.

Reflection

The Spirit of the Sovereign LORD is on me, because the LORD has anointed me to preach good news to the poor (Isaiah 61:1).

SATAN STEALERS OR VICTORY SEALERS

Here we are at the end of our journey together. I can hardly believe we are at the finish line! I pray and trust that God has revealed himself to you in a deeper and more intimate way and that the Holy Spirit has transformed you. That's at least what we are promised when we are intentional about studying and practicing God's Word in our lives.

As we review what God has taught us, it is important to understand that our enemy would like to steal from us the treasures we have mined from God's Word over the past several weeks. So to make sure this doesn't occur, we are going to embark this week on a journey of remembering. We are going to ask God to reveal to us the significant things that we have learned and create memorial markers so we can continue in our growth of obedience in loving God.

Over and over in the Old Testament, God reveals the importance of remembering the events that are significant in following him. Look up the following verses and note why "remembering" was significant to the transpiring events.

Genesis 8:13-22

Genesis 12:1-7

Exodus 24:4-7

Judges 6:11-23

DAY TWO

When God reveals something significant to us, it is important to do everything we can to remember. One of the best ways to do this is to keep a record. The children of Israel erected altars as a reminder to those who passed by of the power of God and his sovereignty.

One way to seal what God has done is to write it down and then punctuate it with a Scripture. I have done this not only in my personal journal but in my Bible as well, noting the date and the significance of what God was teaching me at that time.

Use the following chart over the next two or three days to help you review the ground we've covered. Condensing some of the key thoughts and verses ought to help you bring it all together into a cohesive picture.

Review Chart

Week	Truths Reviewed	Sealing Scriptures
Week 1: **Looking in** **the Mirror**	What significant truths did you learn about veils?	
Week 2: **Celebrating** **the Design**	How did God speak to you about your unique design from Psalm 139? Summarize what you learned from these two lessons and punctuate with Scripture.	

Week	Truths Reviewed	Sealing Scriptures
Week 3: Performance or Purpose	What did you learn about yourself in regard to wearing the veil of performance? According to what you learned through God's Word, what have you purposed to do differently? What are the top three lies you believe about yourself? 1. 2. 3.	What specific Scripture can you use to refute these lies?
Week 4: Secrecy or Transparency	What are you going to do to be more transparent and authentic in your relationships with others and with God? Be specific.	

Week	Truths Reviewed	Sealing Scriptures
Week 5: Darkness or Freedom – Am I Angry?	What did you learn about yourself and the emotion of anger? Be specific. From Ephesians 4:26-31, which of those listed do you need the most help with right now? From James 3:1-12 on page 76, which of the seven deadly poisons of the tongue do you recognize needing the most help with? If you are struggling with forgiveness, which keys (page 78) need the most application right now?	

Week	Truths Reviewed	Sealing Scriptures
Week 6: Darkness or Freedom – Why Do I Feel This Way?	Which character and their depression do you identify with at the moment—Elijah, David, Jonah, or Hannah? Why? What steps can you take to guard yourself against further disappointment and despair?	
Week 7: Freedom to Worship	Summarize what you learned about worship from this study. How has your worship towards God changed as a result of studying during Week Seven?	

Week	Truths Reviewed	Sealing Scriptures
Week 8: Freedom to Love Others	Review the acrostic BUILD (page 111). Which of the five needs the most work in your life? What steps are you going to take to apply what you have learned?	
Week 9: Freedom to Tell Your Story	Who are the people you are going to pray for? What is your plan of action to be intentional about reaching out to those in your sphere of influence?	

DAY FIVE

Many times I have finished a meaningful Bible study and closed the book saying, "Wow!" I learned so much that I was both overwhelmed and paralyzed, feeling unable to apply what I'd learned. I believe the transformational power of studying God's Word and responding to what God has revealed to us comes by following up what we have learned with an action plan. A written plan helps avert our inevitable human tendencies of traveling the same wilderness again and again before truth has been internalized. A plan also helps solidify a commitment or determination to change. But in the process of summarizing, it helps me to remember and then ask God to continue to help me with the journey.

Satan's strategy is to steal what God has done in our hearts. We can counter his thieving ways by remembering and applying God's Word to what we have discovered. I have listed below three victory sealers to prevent the enemy from coming around and sneaking into the camp to steal those treasures. I trust that you will find these helpful as you summarize what God has taught you through this study.

Victory Sealers

- Write down what God has taught you on a 3 x 5 card, in a journal, or in your Bible—put it in a place where it will be a constant reminder of your commitment to follow through.

- Tell someone—be accountable. Ask them to pray with you and check in with you from time to time; join a small group.

- Read—find resources to help you overcome and strengthen yourself against your weakness to sin, such as a workbook, etc.

On the following pages, list the top three things God revealed to you during this study, referring to the chart you have filled out. Summarize each thought, and apply a Scripture that supports this focus. After the summary and Scripture, create an action plan to begin praying and reviewing on a regular basis.

It has been more than joy to walk this journey with you the past several weeks and months. Removing the veils that hinder us from living free in Christ is a daily process. My prayer is that you have seen God's tender and loving hand over your life and his desire for you to experience the depths of his love. May the conclusion of this study be the beginning of a newfound freedom as you uniquely mirror God's glory through your life!

Reflection

And we, who with unveiled faces all reflect the Lord's glory, are being transformed into his likeness with ever-increasing glory, which comes from the Lord, who is the Spirit (2 Corinthians 3:18).

Top Three Truths

Truth #1

Summary of what God has taught me:

Scripture:

Action plan:

Truth #2

Summary of what God has taught me:

Scripture:

Action plan:

Truth #3

Summary of what God has taught me:

Scripture:

Action Plan:

Decade and/or age & themes	Beginnings 0-20	Healing of Pain Gift Discovery 21-25	Children Family 26-29	Ministry 30-32	Reflection 33-36	Transitions 37- 39	New Adventures 40-45	Hi's & Lows 46 to present
Events/People	Salvation with Mom Baptism	Depression/Opression following birth of Jeremy	Infertility struggles – Lisa friend Dr. office Christ, discipled	Pastors Conference: Howard Hendricks Teaching	Major Surgery Sabbatical One year from CDT	Canada Calling and moving	Mom/Sisters PEI trip/healing relationships	Speaking, Book Contracts, Refresh Conferences Grandchildren!!
Events/People	Camping with Family early bonding	Marriage breakdown timeout	Jordan born	Worship Director	Counselling performance issues/family	Illness, Loss of family: Grandpa, Aunt	Marriage struggle/crisis	Cambodia Human Trafficking Vision Trip
Events/People	Grandparents faith stories influenced my view of God	Anger issues explored: Healing and counseling	Jason born	Mentors: Judy/Shirley	Pine Valley Womens Retreat Ministry	Conflict Mom Depression (5 yrs.)	2000: Women's Director	Jordan married
Events/People	Lake Retreat Renewal, revelation of full surrender	Mentors: Pastor Jan/Sharla	Writing first bible study: Women Encouraging Women	Step down from Worship	Death of a Dream Music California	Jeremy: leaves to finish Highschool lives with our best friends	Two more bible studies written Jeremy married	Marriage issues surface
Events/People	Mission Trip: Life Calling for full time ministry	Gifts revealed/emerging and empowered by Kevin and mentors	Grandmothers Illness	CDT Ministry	Family Europe Trip 11 countries Mission/Fun	Jeremy leaves for college	Women Emerge/birthed at Alaska Conf.	Marriage Crisis/Separation FS/Counselling
Events/People	Marriage to Kevin, met on the beach	CDT Ministry Creation	Caregiving of Grandmother		Retreat: Release of performance issues	PW Conference Encouragement	Focus on the Family hired	Enter MAL Program Jason Married Grandchildren!
Events/People	Jeremy born surprise and blessing!	Loss of child			Illness: Pneumonia	Building Together Conferences, Jill Briscoe	2004 Refresh Beth Moore & Leaders	NSM Leadership Development
Events/People						Birthday Trip w/ girlfriends	Death of Dream FF Leadership	Speaking Revival Writing
Lessons	*Faith is Established by Influence*	*Purpose In Pain: new life comes from difficulty*	*Leaving a Legacy: family is a gift*	*Psalm 139: God loves me intimately treasured*	*God doesn't put me in the wilderness to destroy me but develop*	*Knowing Christ deeper and identifying with him*	*God doesn't call the equipped He equips the called*	*Life cycles of great pain forge great blessing*

NOTE: After you list your events/people in each box, shade the box in yellow. The painful events, shade them in pink. The Lessons at the bottom of the chart, shade in blue or green. Be as creative as you like with your headings and lessons.

ACKNOWLEDGMENTS

I began the outline of this project as a book, and then God gently whispered to me to write a Bible study. I started compiling the parts of the journey I had struggled with in dealing with issues of performance, depression, and anger. I wasn't sure I had heard right, but there was a constant, gentle prodding of the Holy Spirit.

I ignored it for nearly a year, in part because I felt so inadequate. Philippians 4:13, "I can do all things through Christ who strengthens me," became a reality as I began to write. This came as no surprise to my copartner on the women's ministry team at the time who exhorted and encouraged me to begin. Thank you, Julie—without your initial words, I might still be outlining a book.

A very special thank you to the women at Cedar Grove Church who wholeheartedly embraced the study. They diligently did all the homework and kept me on target week after week. I appreciated their honest input so the study could have maximum effectiveness.

Thank you to Grace Bible Church in Arroyo Grande, California, and Johnston Heights in Surrey, BC, for piloting the study.

To my awesome first draft editor, Diane Down. I still can't believe that you love to do all the detail work it takes to produce a finished manuscript! Your wisdom and insight have been invaluable. And I appreciated your authentic sharing of your own pathway of growth as we worked through each chapter. I certainly couldn't have completed such a project without you!

To the team at Redemption Press: Project Manager, Hannah; Editors, Barbara and Julie; and the rest of the team who know what it takes to produce an excellent product. And to my friend, Athena, who has continued to cheer me on faithfully with this message of unveiling to help others pursue freedom in Christ. I am grateful.

To my parents, who pray for me continually. To my family, who gave me lots of grace as I was writing—lots of pizza and fast food so I could work long into the evening hours. But mostly, much of what is contained in these pages is the result of my three sons, Jeremy, Jordan, and Jason, walking the path of healing with their mother as they grew up ... thank you, my precious boys, for holding me accountable, giving me lots of love, and reminding me that nobody is perfect and that it is okay to have flaws.

An incredible thank you to my husband, Kevin. You have been my greatest cheerleader in leading me to develop and use my spiritual gifts. You helped me to see the value of sharing my story with others.

And lastly, thanks to my wonderful Lord and Savior Jesus Christ. The giver of life, my redeemer, my God of second chances, my most intimate friend, the one whom I adore and desire to worship with my life. I am daily learning to love you with all of my heart, mind, soul, and strength.

JOURNAL PAGES

JOURNAL PAGES

JOURNAL PAGES

JOURNAL PAGES

JOURNAL PAGES

JOURNAL PAGES

JOURNAL PAGES

JOURNAL PAGES

JOURNAL PAGES

JOURNAL PAGES

JOURNAL PAGES

JOURNAL PAGES

JOURNAL PAGES

JOURNAL PAGES

JOURNAL PAGES

JOURNAL PAGES

JOURNAL PAGES

JOURNAL PAGES

JOURNAL PAGES

JOURNAL PAGES

RESOURCES

Books on Performance and Authenticity

Uninvited: Living Loved When You Feel Less Than, Left Out and Lonely by Lisa Terkeurst

Unashamed: Drop the Baggage, Pick Up Your Freedom, Fulfill Your Destiny by Christine Caine

Abba's Child: The Cry of the Heart For Intimate Belonging by Brennan Manning

Lies Women Believe and the Truth that Sets Them Free by Nancy Leigh DeMoss

Books on Purpose

Without Rival: Embrace Your Identity and Purpose in an Age of Confusion and Comparison by Lisa Bevere

On Mission with God by Henry T. Blackaby

If You Want to Walk on Water, You've Got to Get Out of the Boat by John Ortberg

Books on Anger

Overcoming Emotions That Destroy: Practical Help for Those Angry Feelings That Ruin Relationships by Chip Ingram and Dr. Becca Johnson

Anger: Handling a Powerful Emotion in a Powerful Way by Gary Chapman

She's Gonna Blow: Real Help for Mom's Dealing with Anger by Julie Ann Barnhill

The Anger Workbook by Drs. Les Carter and Frank Minirth

Books on Depression

A Woman's Guide to Overcoming Depression by Archibald Hart and Catherine Weber

Why Do I Feel This Way: What Every Woman Needs to Know About Depression by Brenda Poinsett

Unveiling Depression in Women by Archibald Hart, Catherine Weber Hart

The Freedom from Depression Workbook by Drs. Les Carter and Frank Minirth

Hope Prevails: Insights from a Doctor's Personal Journey through Depression by Dr. Michelle Bengston

Hope Prevails Bible Study: Compassion, Grace, Healing in Your Journey Through Depression by Dr. Michelle Bengston

Books on Worship

Extravagant Worship by Darlene Zchech

Worshipping God: Devoting our Lives to His Glory by R.T. Kendall

Books on Telling Your Story

To Be Told: Know Your Story, Shape Your Future by Dan Allender

Speak: How Your Story Can Change the World by Nish Weiseth

Devotional and Prayer Books

New Morning Mercies: A Daily Gospel Devotional by Paul David Tripp

A Very Present Help by Amy Carmichael

My Utmost For His Highest by Oswald Chambers

Prayer That Works by Jill Briscoe

Praying God's Word by Beth Moore

For further Study on Spiritual Gifts:

Understanding Spiritual Gifts by Kay Arthur, David Lawson and B.J. Lawson

Free gift test online:

http://www.lifeway.com/Article/Women-Leadership-Spiritual-gifts-growth-service

ORDER INFORMATION

To order additional copies of this book, please visit
www.redemption-press.com.
Also available on Amazon.com and BarnesandNoble.com
Or by calling toll free 1-844-2REDEEM.

CPSIA information can be obtained
at www.ICGtesting.com
Printed in the USA
BVHW090040230719
554057BV00015B/747/P

9 781683 142461